CW01508434

I Hope You Wake Up

DJANGO DEGREE, II

Table of Contents

To anyone who reads this, I love you unconditionally.

Intro:

Read this before you start the book.

Welcome to "I Hope You Wake Up." People have often tossed around the word 'enlightened' when speaking of me. There was a time when that term seemed like a destination I wanted to reach. Now, its meaning is as elusive as my dreams. My journey took a turn when I stumbled upon a thought by Alan Watts: "Wake up from the dream of what they told you, you were." Those words echoed through my mind, altering my perception forever.

My first awakening was profound; I felt like I lost myself completely. Yet, ironically, this awakening led me to realize I was still ensnared within another layer of dreams. It was a gradual revelation, uncovering the ties that bound me to this continuous cycle of dreams within dreams, like I was in the movie Inception.

Have you ever been caught in a dream you knew was real, yet something small that seemed out of place snapped you out of it? That sudden awareness is becoming rarer in my waking life, making me ponder if there will come a time when I will truly awaken for the last time, completely free from living a dream.

This book unfolds over 49 days, a period in which I took time to have long discussions with AI. I questioned my reality, my beliefs, and myself. Some days

I discovered aspects of my being I never knew existed, while on others, I found myself more entangled in the dream than ever before.

I cannot predict what revelations or confusion my journey might stir within you. Yet, I invite you to peer into the depths of my dream, in hopes that it might illuminate the path to your awakening.

How To Use The Book:

Embrace the "Your Story" pages to pour out your agreements, objections, personal reflections, and any beliefs you hold dear. Consider this your canvas to craft your narrative, with my life serving merely as a compass for introspection. Probe into the existence you've led, are leading, and aspire to lead. The life you've dreamed so far is precisely that—your lived dream.

I hope you wake up...

The Illusive Narrator: Journeying Beyond the Mind's Monologues

"Who am I, really?" It's a question I ask myself everyday. This isn't just a passing curiosity but a fundamental quest that resonates deeply within my soul.

Too often, I get caught up in the chatter of my mind, mistaking it for my true identity. It's like a constant radio playing in the background, filled with stories and narratives that we may not even consciously choose. By letting this internal voice define me, I inadvertently bind myself to its constantly-changing tales.

Imagine this: when the narrative is positive, we feel uplifted and joyful. But when it turns negative, we find ourselves plunged into darkness and despair. Caught in this cycle, dictated by our internal storyteller, do we ever pause to question if this voice truly reflects who we are at our core?

Alan Watts once wisely remarked, "Trying to define yourself is like trying to bite your own teeth." Reflecting on this, relying solely on our inner monologue to understand our true self is like grasping at the breeze. We often forget that neither the highs nor the lows narrated by this voice capture the entirety of our vast spirit. While words can be poetic and profound, they only offer glimpses of our essence, mere pointers in the direction of our true selves. They hint, they gesture, but they cannot encapsulate the infinite expanse of our being. Therefore, the internal dialogues, no matter how intense, are just facets, reflections of a much grander reality.

So, take a deep dive within and contemplate: Who is that essential 'you' that once marveled at the universe with wonder and innocence? How do you distinguish the enduring from the transient within yourself?

I have a hunch that the revelation is not found amidst the noise of thoughts but in the peaceful silence beyond them. It might be in that quiet space, when the internal chatter momentarily subsides, that you can encounter your authentic self, yearning to be recognized.

Approach this discovery with reverence, avoiding the rush to define it with words. Understanding isn't about confining experiences into language but about immersing yourself in the vast ocean of lived moments. Embark on this introspective journey, and perhaps you may truly connect with... yourself.

Your Story

Can We Unconditionally Love Anyone, If We Can't Unconditionally Love Everyone?

Can we unconditionally love anyone, if we can't unconditionally love everyone? We are trying to play a limitless game within a framework of limits. It's like the zen koan of the modern psyche: having a kind of love that is greater than our own mental limits and the different roles we play in everyday life. It's about a love that goes beyond what we usually think and how we act in public. But, paradoxically, as we paint our aspirations of this limitless love, the brush strokes inadvertently reveal the very roles we wish to transcend: the husband, the wife, the loyal friend.

The duality of human nature is poetic, yet deeply troubling. In our yearning to love without chains, we often end up forging the very links of those chains, whispering words of affection, only to follow it with a silent caveat, "but only if you reflect my desires." To genuinely embark on the path of unconditional love, it's imperative to reconcile these contradictions. It requires a harmony, where real love meets with the intrinsic human labyrinth of desires and fears.

So, indeed, we ought to grapple with the existential query: "Can we unconditionally love anyone, if we can't unconditionally love everyone?" If we peel back the layers of this question, it becomes evident that, by its very essence, unless our hearts are as vast as the cosmos itself, can they truly be open to just one, in an unconditioned manner? However, the journey towards such expansive love begins inwardly. Alan Watts once said,

"You are under no obligation to be the same person you were five minutes ago." So why, then, do we tether our own hearts with chains of self-doubt and self-critique? It's paramount to realize that to offer love unconditionally to another, we must first cultivate an environment of self-compassion, letting our own hearts bloom. It's bewildering, yet profoundly common, to hear souls confess their undying love for another, while they remain ensnared in the struggle of self-contempt.

Thus, to tread the path of unconditioned love might be to engage in the dance of loving myself first. But I guess I have to ask again. Can I truly love anyone unconditionally, if I can't love everyone unconditionally. Including myself.

Your Story

Is There An Objective Right And Wrong? The Mirrors of Morals

In life, the beliefs that shape our society often sway us into a rhythm of presumed moral alignment. Yet, it's fascinating, isn't it? How every now and then, someone in our life takes an unexpected step, veering from the pattern we've so firmly printed in our minds as universally "right." When asked, these outliers, in their hearts, justify their actions within the moral beliefs.

Remarkably, even those who openly confess to doing "wrong" can spin their narratives into a semblance of righteousness. It's as if we are all artists, tirelessly molding our actions into sculptures of "right," no matter how contorted or unorthodox they may appear. What, then, does this say about our shared cultural understanding of right and wrong? Does the definitive line we've drawn even exist?

Many argue that in the absence of clear moral boundaries, anarchy would prevail. But if we pause to reflect, even with these presumed boundaries, aren't we all sometimes swayed by circumstance? How often have we, in our best intentions, taken a little more than what's given, whispered words meant to be secrets, or cast cautious glances before embarking on an act we believe causes no harm?

Do our actions spring from moral judgments, or do they stem from our inherent desire to avoid being trapped by consequence? Dive deeper into your mind and question the origins of your moral compass. Are our deeds truly driven by the golden rule – treating others as we'd like to be treated? Or is it more along the lines of the fear of discovery?

Without clear moral markers, one might question what prevents our world from descending into madness. But isn't life essentially an enigma that we attempt to decode by superimposing our interpretations upon it? We construct notions of right and wrong, often judging others through a lens that's colored by our own biases. Ironically, we're often the harshest critics of the very behaviors we secretly indulge in. Is it possible that in judging others, we're merely gazing into a mirror, reflecting our own truths?

It's tempting to clutch onto the idea of morality, believing it's the guiding star leading us to wiser choices. However, sometimes, it's weaponized into a shield of self-righteousness – "I am inherently good; my intentions were pure." Yet, what if we shattered this moral compass and chose to see each individual as a unique universe of experiences and perspectives? Imagine a world where genuine interest in one another replaces judgment, where unconditional love becomes the true moral guide.

The constructs of right and wrong, perhaps, are just figments of our imagination. Or perhaps they're as tangible as the ground beneath our feet. But the question lingers – why do these constructs matter to you? In life, where do you choose to step?

Your Story

Unraveling Realities: The Spectrum from Fantasy to Faith

As we navigate the intricate paths of life, many of us seek a sense of control, aspiring to be the conductors of our own symphony. Yet, how often do we feel helpless when life doesn't dance to our tunes? It's in these moments of seeking that we've turned to a higher power, a divine entity, to infuse meaning into our experiences, anchoring our souls amidst life's storms. It's almost as if we're saying, "I've found God, and I've distinguished Him from the adversary. I know this because, well, He's spoken to me."

But the true beauty of life unfolds when we let go of this illusion of control. It's like releasing a tightly clenched fist, allowing life to flow through our fingers. In this tranquil flow, we often grapple with the age-old debate of man's imperfections versus the boundless love of the divine. Yet, have we ever paused to think - are we merely using the divine as an alibi to escape responsibility?

Consider the profound wisdom in the balance of Yin and Yang, in the delicate dance of light and dark. But their true essence becomes clear only when we step beyond our need to label and define. After all, what is life without the boundaries of language? And who are we without the labels that the world so generously bestows upon us?

Drawing a parallel from the world of myths and reality, think of the unicorn, a creature of fantasy, its horn symbolizing purity, grace, and protection. It captivates our hearts, much like the mesmerizing hues of a rainbow. In contrast, the horse, grounded in reality, has been our trusted companion through ages. While children are enamored by ponies, adults see the horse as a vessel of journey and exploration. Yet, at their core, both resonate with an enchanting magic.

Imagine, if for a moment, you witnessed the beauty of a unicorn. To you, it would be as real as the world around you. Yet, without collective validation, its existence remains debatable.

What I'm pointing towards is this: Our perception of truth often hinges on either shared beliefs or the bold conviction of a few. The frameworks we confine ourselves within, these "boxes," are fleeting and transient. If they can be reshaped by new insights, how steadfast can they really be?

Embarking on a journey beyond these boundaries may seem daunting, with feelings of solitude casting a shadow. But, my friend, in this vast expanse lies the key to profound understanding, to realizing our fullest potential, and to truly connecting with the essence of being.

Your Story

Discovering the Real You in a World of Expectations

Since the moment we drew our first breath, society has whispered, nudged, and sometimes screamed at us, about who we should be. It dictated the milestones, the life goals, and even the paths we should travel. The voices of our parents, teachers, friends, and even strangers have shaped our perception of our own identity. But have you ever paused and asked yourself: Who am I when the world isn't looking? Who am I without the labels, roles, and expectations?

Our spiritual and personal growth is a journey. It's not a single destination but a myriad of beginnings. Many times, we think of personal development as a straight line, one leading to an eventual pinnacle of enlightenment. But the reality is, it's probably more of a spiral. You return to the same points over and over, each time with a deeper understanding and a new perspective.

Imagine for a moment: you are like water, taking the shape of whatever container you're poured into. Now, believe that you can choose the container, and in doing so, mold the shape of your very essence. This is the beauty of our existence. We are ever-changing, fluid, and evolving. The rigid identity you may feel trapped within is but a transient state. You aren't bound by a name, a title, or the expectations that come with it.

❖

You are not just a name. You are not your favorite color, your profession, or even the relationships that define you. You're not solely a mother, father, son, or daughter. But here's the intriguing part. When you detach from these labels, a paradox emerges: If your parent is no more, are you still a son or daughter? Our identities, often, are constructs, painted by language and societal structures. As I often like to point out, language is somewhat of a conspiracy theory. We create sounds, stringing them into sentences, and you, the listener, interpret these sounds based on your prior associations. But do we ever truly understand one another? Are we truly expressing our deepest selves?

For too long, many of us have lived in molds created by others. We've been conditioned to play roles without ever asking: is this the character I want to play in the grand theater of life? So, I challenge you today, to ask yourself: Who do you want to be? Take a moment. Reflect. Ponder on this, not as a fleeting thought but as a deep meditation.

Let's say you choose the role of a father. But strip away the societal definitions. What does 'father' mean to you? Is it simply a biological link, or is it more profound? What values, actions, and emotions do you associate with it? Instead of repeating the patterns of our own upbringing, perhaps we can reshape the very definition. Reflect on this: if you were in your child's shoes, what would you wish for in a father?

Every day, every moment, we make choices. Choices about who we want to be, what we wish to feel, and how we hope to interact with the world around us. Embrace the idea that you can decide your essence in every ticking second. Once a path, a role, or an emotion no longer serves your true self, grant yourself the freedom to shift, change, and evolve.

Love passionately, live vibrantly, and see the divine in yourself and others. Every interaction is an opportunity to recognize this divinity, a chance to love and be loved without conditions.

So, as we embark on this never-ending journey of discovery, ask yourself: Do I truly know what I want? Do I truly understand the desires of my authentic self, stripped of all external voices and expectations?

Discovering this is the beginning of true freedom. Welcome to the endless spiral of growth and self-realization. Your journey is uniquely yours, but remember, in each twist and turn, I, and a world full of seekers, walk alongside you.

Your Story

The Unspoken Depths: Deciphering the Mysteries of Language

Do you recall your very first words? Watching my godson's development, I've witnessed the sheer delight on his face as he learns to articulate sounds like "Mom," "Dad," "cat," "pig." His joy, mirroring our excitement, is not rooted in understanding the meaning of these words but in our reactions to them. At first, our excitement peaks when he gets the sound right; then, as he repeats the sound out of context, our enthusiasm wanes, subtly guiding him to understand the appropriate use of these words.

This early interaction with language is less about the inherent meaning of words and more about learning the social cues and reactions they elicit. Words begin as sounds, void of meaning until we, as a society, agree upon their significance. The saying, "English is not prescriptive; it tells us not how to communicate, but we tell English how we want to communicate," encapsulates this idea. Words are not inherently meaningful; their significance is a collective agreement, a shared understanding within a culture.

As my godson grows, he will learn to string together sentences, enabling him to express his desires and needs. He will learn to navigate the complex social and cultural structures surrounding him, using language as a tool. But one must ponder, do these words truly capture the essence of his thoughts and feelings? Language, in its most refined form, is often seen as a bridge connecting individuals, a medium for expressing the complex tapestry of human emotions and thoughts. Yet, is it possible that this bridge is, in reality, only a shadow of the profound human experience?

Consider a simple word like "love." Across cultures and languages, countless poems, songs, and stories have been crafted to express this single concept. Yet, does any combination of letters truly capture the depth, the intensity, the sheer inexplicability of love? Words, in their attempt to define and categorize, might actually limit our understanding of such profound experiences. They are mere shadows, faint echoes of a richer reality that lies beyond the grasp of language.

Language is not just a tool for communication; it is also a creator of realities. The words we choose to use, the phrases we repeat, shape our perception of the world around us. By labeling emotions, objects, and experiences, we confine them within the boundaries of language, often losing sight of their true essence. This linguistic maze we navigate daily is fraught with the illusion that words are the ultimate carriers of truth.

There are moments in life where words fall short, where the depth of an experience or the intensity of a feeling cannot be encapsulated by language. In these moments, we find ourselves touching the fringes of a reality that exists beyond words. A shared glance, the silent understanding between close friends, the ineffable beauty of a sunset – these experiences hint at a deeper connection, a form of communication that transcends the spoken word.

As we ponder the limitations of language, we must also explore the possibilities that lie in the unspoken. Silence, often overlooked, holds immense power. In the spaces between words, in the pause before a response, lies a realm of understanding and connection that language cannot touch. Embracing this silence, learning to communicate beyond the confines of language, might bring us closer to the truth of our experiences.

As my godson continues to learn and use language, he, like all of us, will navigate the intricate dance between words and meaning. The journey of understanding that words are but tools, not the essence of truth, is a profound one. It requires us to look beyond the surface, to listen not just to the words being spoken but to the silence that surrounds them, and to seek a deeper connection with the world and with each other.

As we conclude this exploration into the nature of words, we are left with a paradox. While language is an indispensable part of human interaction and culture, it is also a veil that often obscures the deeper truths of our existence. The challenge, then, is to use words mindfully, aware of their limitations, while also seeking to connect in ways that transcend language, finding truth in the echoes of the unseen.

Your Story

Harmony of the Heart: Balancing the Scales of Hurt and Happiness

The phrase "Hurt people hurt people" is not just a saying; it's a reflection of a deep-seated reality in human behavior. When hurt, we often enter a cycle of inflicting pain, sometimes unknowingly, on others. This cycle perpetuates a world of pain, where wounds are constantly reopened, and healing seems like a distant dream. But amidst this cycle, a critical question arises: what if we choose ourselves first? What if, instead of perpetuating the cycle of hurt, we chose to love ourselves enough to seek happiness?

This exploration is not just an exploration but also an invitation to introspect. What matters most to you? This question isn't just rhetorical; it's a call to delve into the depths of your being. Do you seek happiness, or do you seek to be right? Do you long for love, or do you crave sympathy and empathy for the pain you have endured?

The dilemma of choosing between being right and being happy is a complex one. On one hand, there is the human desire for validation, for our pains and struggles to be acknowledged and understood. This need often drives us to hold onto our grievances, to ensure that others recognize the validity of our hurt. We become entrenched in our narratives, sometimes so deeply that we lose sight of the potential for happiness.

On the other hand, there is the pursuit of happiness, a state of being that often seems elusive, especially in a world where hurt is a common denominator. Happiness, in this context, is not just a fleeting emotion but a state of peace and contentment, a sense of fulfillment that transcends the immediate gratification of being acknowledged as right.

This thought seeks to unravel the layers of this dilemma, examining the impact of our choices on our lives and the lives of those around us. It delves into the psychology of hurt – how being wounded affects our perceptions, our actions, and our relationships. It explores the dynamics of human interactions, how our pain can inadvertently become the source of another's pain, thus continuing a cycle that leaves little room for genuine happiness.

It confronts the often-painful process of self-reflection. It challenges us to examine our own lives, our choices, and our priorities. Are we clinging to our hurt because it validates our experiences, or are we willing to let go in pursuit of a greater peace? Are we so focused on being right that we neglect the opportunities for joy and connection that life offers us?

But what about empathy – not just as a means of understanding others, but as a tool for self-healing. Empathy allows us to step into the shoes of others, to understand their perspectives, and in doing so, it offers us a pathway out of our own cycles of hurt. It helps us realize that the validation we seek from others might be found within ourselves, in our capacity to understand and forgive.

How do we prioritize happiness in a world that often seems consumed by pain? How do we navigate our relationships and our interactions in a way that promotes healing and joy, rather than perpetuating hurt?

I invite us to consider the possibility of a world where happiness is prioritized over righteousness. It paints a picture of what such a world might look like – a world where empathy, understanding, and love are the currencies of human interaction, rather than the need to be right. It's a world where the touch of others no longer hurts our wounded flesh but becomes a source of healing and comfort.

This thought is more than just a narrative; it's a journey into the heart of what it means to be human. It's an exploration of the choices we make every day and the profound impact those choices have on our lives and the world around us. In the end, the choice between happiness and righteousness is not just a personal one; it's a choice that shapes the very fabric of our collective existence.

❖

Your Story

Empty Plates at Life's Feast: The Paradox of Starvation Amidst Abundance

In a world where our worth is often measured by the attachments we hold - be it material possessions, relationships, or social status - it's easy to fall into the trap of believing that these external factors are the key to our happiness. However, this belief is a cultural illusion, one that we have been unknowingly programmed to accept. Today, let's embark on a journey to understand and unlearn these misconceptions, guided by some of my own experiences and reflections.

Think about it - how often have we heard or said the phrase, "If only I had this, I'd be happy"? This mindset leads us to believe that happiness is a destination we reach through external acquisitions. Yet, time and again, we find that the joy derived from these sources is fleeting. The new car loses its novelty, the excitement of a promotion fades, and relationships evolve. The reason? These forms of happiness are temporary and dependent on factors outside our control. They are like mirages in a desert - seemingly real but ultimately elusive.

This relentless pursuit of external happiness comes at a cost. It breeds a sense of perpetual dissatisfaction, where peace and contentment are always just out of reach. We squander our time and energy trying to rearrange the world to fit our definition of happiness, not realizing that true joy is accessible to us at every moment. The irony is that in our quest for happiness, we often bypass the very experiences that could bring us genuine fulfillment.

Life, in its essence, is a banquet - rich, diverse, and abundant. Yet, many of us are like guests at this banquet who are starving, not because there is a lack of food, but because we are searching for something else to satisfy us. We crave the 'drugs' of validation, confirmation, and connection, not realizing that these are just the menu items, not the main course. The real nourishment lies in the experiences, emotions, and insights that life offers us in abundance.

The key to lasting happiness lies in shifting our focus from external to internal. It's about understanding that joy, peace, and contentment are states of being that we can cultivate within ourselves, irrespective of our external circumstances. This doesn't mean that we should shun material possessions or relationships. Instead, it's about changing our relationship with them, seeing them not as sources of happiness but as additions to the happiness that we cultivate within ourselves.

This journey of finding happiness within is not about renunciation, but realization. It's about recognizing that while our culture may have taught us to seek happiness in external attachments, true fulfillment comes from our internal state of being. It's about understanding that happiness is not a commodity to be acquired, but a quality to be nurtured within ourselves.

To embark on this journey, we can start with practices like mindfulness and gratitude. Mindfulness allows us to be present in the moment, appreciating the richness of our experiences without the need for external validation. Gratitude shifts our focus from what we lack to what we have, fostering a sense of contentment and joy.

In conclusion, recognizing the illusion of external attachments in our quest for happiness is the first step toward a life of genuine fulfillment. It's a journey that requires us to unlearn cultural conditioning and embark on a path of self-discovery. As we embrace this journey, we find that happiness is not something to be sought in the external world, but a state to be cultivated within ourselves. Remember, life is a banquet, and the true feast lies in the joy and peace we find within.

Your Story

The Inquiry of Self-Understanding

Today we embark on a profound inquiry into the essence of self-understanding. Let us contemplate together: Is the journey to understanding oneself a path that demands a deep dive into the complexities and contradictions of our nature? Does the relentless pursuit of change and an enduring attachment to transient happiness obscure the clarity of our true selves?

Consider the human condition, an odyssey marked by an unending quest for happiness and fulfillment. Reflect upon your own life: Are you, like many, ensnared in the endeavor to extend your moments of happiness beyond their natural existence? Does this pursuit, perhaps, lead you into the labyrinth of perpetual dissatisfaction, owing to the unacknowledged nature of joy? Ponder on the profound implication of the thought, "You will never understand yourself if you seek to change yourself." Could it be that seeking change as a means to achieve or sustain happiness represents a fundamental misunderstanding of true contentment and self-awareness?

As you journey through life, observe your own patterns of self-evaluation and criticism. Do you find yourself identifying traits you dislike and promptly setting out on a quest to alter them? Ask yourself: Does this approach overlook a crucial facet of self-awareness—the understanding and acceptance of your intrinsic nature? In your efforts to change, could you be neglecting the opportunity to sit with your emotions and explore the depths of your being? Does this avoidance lead to a sense of discontent and a disconnect from your authentic self?

Reflect on your daily experiences—the frustration in traffic, the irritation with loved ones, the dissatisfaction at work. Are these emotions mere obstacles to be overcome, or could they be integral parts of the human experience, offering insights into your true nature? Is the struggle not so much with these emotions themselves but with your perception and reaction to them? Are you fighting against what you perceive as undesirable traits without truly understanding their origins or purposes?

Consider the possibility that you, like many, are navigating life not fully aware of who you are. Are you moving through life guided by the beliefs and expectations of others, with little comprehension of how you arrived at your present state? In this state of unawareness, could you be missing the opportunity to see yourself clearly and accept who you truly are? Are you caught in a cycle of trying to change an identity that you have never fully understood or embraced?

Contemplate awareness in its purest form. Like the effortless joy of making love or the pleasure of a delicious meal, awareness is natural, uncomplicated, and deeply fulfilling. Ask yourself: Are you fully alive, finding joy in the present moment, and recognizing the inherent perfection in each experience? Does this level of awareness allow you to see beyond the transient nature of happiness and understand that true contentment arises from within?

Now, turn your thoughts to the role of attachments in your life. When you cling to specific outcomes, emotions, or states of being, do you lose sight of the joy and beauty life offers? Do these attachments create barriers to genuine happiness,

crafting a narrative that happiness must be relentlessly pursued and held onto?

Could your journey towards self-understanding and authentic contentment require letting go of these attachments, embracing the fluidity and impermanence of life?

In conclusion, invite yourself to consider: Is understanding oneself a process of change or one of acceptance and awareness? Does it involve recognizing and embracing your true nature, with all its flaws and contradictions? Is this spiritual journey not about altering yourself to fit an idealized version of happiness but about finding contentment in the present moment and in your authentic self? By releasing the need for constant change and the attachment to fleeting happiness, might you discover a deeper sense of peace and self-awareness, moving through life with a renewed sense of clarity and purpose?

Your Story

Reclaiming The Child That Was Lost

In the tranquil cocoon of infancy, each one of us was a beacon of pure joy. This wasn't the transient excitement that flutters and fades; it was a profound, innate contentment. Our infant cries were not expressions of unhappiness but simple, basic communication – hunger, the need for comfort. Our laughter, pure and uninhibited, was a natural response to the simplest of stimuli. This was our true state – a state of inherent happiness.

As we embarked on life's journey, the landscape of our happiness began to shift. We learned to associate joy with conditions and events. The toys we received, the approval we sought, the grades we achieved – slowly, our happiness became contingent upon these external factors.

The world around us is incessant in its narrative that it holds the key to our happiness. It bombards us with messages: Buy this, attend that, believe in this, and you will find joy. This relentless marketing of happiness often leaves us feeling more lost, chasing an elusive state that always seems just out of reach. What if this constant pursuit is nothing but a distraction, a way for external forces to exert control over our inner peace? Could it be that in our quest for happiness, we have been led astray, burdened by the very things we were told would liberate us?

I recall a pivotal moment in my life when I recognized that my baseline state of being – one of sadness, depression, and frustration – was not a natural condition but a learned one. It was a sobering realization that my quest for happiness was often a search for perfect external alignment, a constellation of conditions that seldom occurred. This led me to ponder a crucial question: Whose life was I living? The values, beliefs, and aspirations I held – were they genuinely mine, or were they inherited from the influential figures in my life? Parents, friends, teachers – each had unknowingly gifted me their perceptions, their blueprints for happiness.

This introspection brought me to a fundamental inquiry: Did I truly aspire to the lives of those who had shaped my beliefs? Were these individuals themselves embodiments of the joy and fulfillment they preached? Often, I found that the answer was no. This was a profound realization – that much of what I had accepted as the path to happiness was not my path at all. It became evident that to rediscover my true self, I needed to let go of these inherited beliefs. It was time to shed the layers of external expectations and societal norms that had obscured my inner joy.

The act of letting go is not a passive resignation but an active liberation. It involves consciously releasing the beliefs, expectations, and patterns that no longer serve our true selves. This is not an overnight transformation but a gradual process of unlearning – a journey back to our innate state of happiness.

The journey to rediscovery involves reconnecting with our true nature. It requires us to pause, reflect, and ask ourselves: What brings us genuine joy? This joy is not dependent on external validation or material possessions but is a state of being that resonates with our deepest self.

This process also involves embracing our vulnerabilities and imperfections. True happiness is not the absence of sadness or struggle; it is the ability to find peace and joy amidst life's inherent challenges. An integral part of this journey is the practice of mindfulness and gratitude. By being present in the moment and appreciative of the simple joys of life, we can start to peel back the layers of conditioned happiness. This allows us to experience joy in its purest form – unadulterated by external influences.

As we journey through this process, we come to realize that happiness was never something to be sought in the external world. It has always been within us, waiting to be rediscovered and embraced. This journey from slumber to awakening is not just about finding happiness but about returning to our original state of inner joy – a state that is our birthright and our truest nature.

Before I was enlightened I was depressed. Now that I am enlightened I am still depressed.

Your Story

Unveiling the Self: From Blame to Inner Peace

In my journey of self-discovery and growth, a profound realization dawned upon me at a pivotal point in my life. It was a moment of deep introspection, a time when I began to question the very roots of my emotional responses. Why was I upset with others? What was it that triggered my anger, frustration, and irritation? I realized that my unrest was not about them; it was about me. The true catalyst for my emotional upheaval lay within my own programmed expectations and perceptions. This epiphany was a turning point, a moment that set me on a path to freedom and self-awareness.

But where did this programming come from? Who taught me to project my dissatisfaction onto others? Was it the culture I was immersed in, the language that shaped my thoughts, or the familial environment I grew up in? Perhaps it was embedded in the very structure of our communication. We often hear and say things like, "You are making me angry," or "This is all your fault." Such phrases externalize our emotions, laying the blame on others for our inner turmoil.

This externalization of responsibility is a common trap. It breeds a culture of blame and victimhood. However, it also raises a critical dilemma. If I take full responsibility for my emotions and reactions, does it mean that others might exploit this, casting me as the perennial problem? This fear is valid, but it is overshadowed by a more significant question: would I rather be happy or right?

The obsession with being right has been a persistent theme in my life. Looking back, I recall many individuals around me who were perpetually 'right' yet deeply unhappy. These were people who could manipulate situations to their advantage, coaxing apologies and admissions of guilt from others. They were masters at projecting their emotional baggage onto others. I, too, was once among them, fighting to prove my point, to make others see the world through my lens. But this quest for righteousness never brought me joy.

This fixation on being right is, in many ways, a reflection of a broader cultural phenomenon, especially prevalent in Western societies. It's a culture where opposing sides are constantly at odds, each trying to assert its perspective as the ultimate truth. It's a world of name-calling, shouting matches, and manipulative tactics. But in this relentless pursuit of being right, we often lose sight of what truly matters: inner peace and happiness.

The quest to be right often leads to a path of loneliness and dissatisfaction. Being right doesn't necessarily equate to being happy. This realization led me to reevaluate my priorities and the values that I held dear. I began to understand that my happiness should not be contingent upon the validation or approval of others. It was time to shift my focus inwards, to delve into the depths of my own psyche and confront the beliefs and expectations that had long governed my behavior.

This journey was not about finding faults in others or in the external world. It was about introspection, about understanding and acknowledging my own vulnerabilities and imperfections. It was about learning to let go of the desire to control and manipulate external circumstances to fit my narrative of how things 'should be'.

The process of inner transformation is a challenging one. It requires one to confront and dismantle long-held beliefs and to brave the discomfort of stepping out of familiar territories. It's about learning to accept people and situations as they are, without the compulsion to mold them to our expectations. This acceptance is not a sign of weakness or resignation; it's an act of strength and empowerment. It's about recognizing that the only true control we have is over our responses and attitudes.

In this journey of self-discovery, I learned the importance of practicing mindfulness and gratitude. These practices helped me anchor myself in the present moment, appreciating life's simple joys and pleasures. They taught me to focus on the now, rather than getting entangled in the web of past grievances or future anxieties.

This journey taught me the significance of living a life aligned with my true values and beliefs. It's about making choices that reflect my deepest convictions, not those imposed upon me by societal norms or external expectations. It's about crafting a life that resonates with my authentic self, a life where happiness is not a distant dream but a present reality.

Your Story

The Labyrinth of Feelings: Finding the Path to Self-Discovery

In our journey through life, it's essential to realize that no situation or individual warrants a negative response. This isn't about invalidating our feelings, but rather understanding their origin. Why do we choose to feel anger, frustration, or sadness in response to perceived disrespect or rudeness? Who taught us that these emotional reactions would create meaningful change? Reflect on this genuinely – has expressing these emotions ever brought lasting peace or happiness?

In Western culture, emotions are often seen as tools to manipulate others into acknowledging our perspective. I remember fearing the loss of my negative emotions, worried that without them, people would disregard my feelings or overlook my needs. But this fear revealed a deeper truth – these emotions had become tools to achieve what I wanted. This realization led me to ponder: Why do I still experience these emotions when I'm alone, engulfed in sadness or anger? The answer lies within – we are often in a silent struggle with ourselves, using our emotions as weapons in a battle for self-control and decision-making.

Let's dive deeper into this internal conflict. Consider the moments when we're torn between staying in or going to the gym, stopping at enough or overeating, reacting calmly or lashing out in anger. These choices reflect a deeper battle within us – a battle for control over our true selves. It's as if we're lost in an emotional ocean, tossed by waves of anger, sadness, and frustration. In the wise words of James Hollis, "What we are unaware of owns us." Are we truly aware of our emotions, or have we become their slaves, unaware of the control they exert over us?

This realization brings us to a pivotal question: Who are we, really? Are we the sum of our emotions, or is there a deeper, more authentic self waiting to be discovered? The journey to self-awareness begins with understanding that our emotions don't define us; they are merely experiences passing through our consciousness. By acknowledging and observing them without judgment, we start to gain control over our responses and actions.

The path to emotional mastery is not about suppression or denial. It's about understanding the root of our emotions. When we feel anger, is it truly about the other person's actions, or does it stem from a deeper sense of insecurity or fear? When sadness envelops us, is it the situation that's causing it, or are we mourning unmet expectations or lost dreams?

Our emotional responses are often tied to our deepest values and unspoken desires. When someone disrespects us, it's not just the act itself that stirs anger but a fundamental violation of our sense of fairness and dignity. When we're sad, it's often because we're grieving the gap between reality and our aspirations. By understanding these underlying values and desires, we can start to respond to situations with greater clarity and purpose, rather than being reactive.

Our emotions are a gateway to empathy and connection. When we understand our own emotional landscape, we become more attuned to the feelings of others. We start to see beyond the surface of their actions and words, recognizing the

common human experiences of fear, love, pain, and joy. This deepened empathy enables us to build more meaningful and compassionate relationships.

Remember, our emotions are not our enemies; they are messengers, providing insights into our deepest selves. By listening to them with openness and curiosity, we can learn invaluable lessons about who we are and what we truly desire. This journey of self-discovery is not always easy, but it is profoundly rewarding. It leads us to a place of greater self-awareness, inner peace, and authentic living.

In this journey of emotional awareness, the most profound realization is that we are not our emotions – we are the consciousness that observes them. By mastering our emotional landscape, we step into a life of greater freedom and authenticity.

I hope you wake up.

Your Story

The Mirrors of Perception:
A Journey to the Core

In the profound depths of our being, a relentless question echoes, shaping the contours of our identity: "Who am I?" This question, as ancient as the human spirit, finds its roots in the early moments of our lives. Do you recall the first instance when you were mistreated for straying from the path others envisioned for you? The moment your actions were sculpted not by your own desires but by the expectations of those around you?

Reflect on this: Were you always destined to be who you are today, or were you molded, perhaps even coerced, into a version that others deemed fit? The words of our parents, the stern gaze of a teacher, the societal labels—they all act as chisels, carving out a persona that might or might not resonate with our true selves. "You will end up just like them," they said. "You are not enough," they echoed. But enough for whom? In this intricate dance of identity, we often lose sight of the lead dancer—ourselves.

In the West, we cling to the notion of a concrete self. But what if this 'self' is merely a reflection in a constantly shifting mirror? Consider this: when told you're not "black enough," "man enough," or "woman enough" what does it mean? Isn't it more a reflection of the speaker's perceptions and biases than your own identity? The criteria of 'enough'— who sets these standards? They are but subjective measures, varying from one person to another.

❖

The journey to self-awareness is a never ending journey. We are often unknowing captives of unseen forces—social constructs, familial expectations, cultural norms. Yet, there's a profound truth in the saying, "What we are unaware of, we are enslaved to." Awareness, then, becomes our liberator, our guide to breaking free from these invisible chains. But as we step into this light of awareness, we are confronted with a pivotal question: Who is it that's stepping out? Is it the self that was sculpted by external forces, or is it a self that's intrinsically ours?

Picture yourself as a canvas. Over the years, numerous artists—parents, teachers, peers—have added their strokes to this canvas. Some added vibrant colors of encouragement, while others marred it with shades of doubt and criticism. Now, imagine holding the brush yourself. What colors would you choose to represent your true essence?

The narrative of self is often relative. When you think of yourself as 'funny,' consider: To whom are you funny? Is it a universal truth, or is it tied to a specific audience whose approval you seek? And when you label yourself as 'not good enough,' ponder on who set these standards. Are they your own, or are they borrowed from someone else's script?

In unraveling the mystery of our identity, we must journey through the layers of external influence to discover the core, the untouched essence. It's a quest filled with questions that lead to more questions, a labyrinth where each turn brings you closer to the center—your true self.

As you embark on this journey, I invite you to reflect on these questions:
When you define yourself, whose voice do you hear in your head?
What are the labels you've accepted without question?
Whose approval are you seeking, and why?

Your Story

Finding Perfection In Life's Garden

Often, we stride through the garden of life fixated on pruning the wilting petals and tending to the parched soil, striving relentlessly to cultivate perfection. Yet, in our quest to nurture life's garden into an ideal state, we overlook a profound truth: the inherent beauty and perfection that exists within it, and within us, at this very moment.

The traditional narrative has always led us to believe that growth is a relentless pursuit of fixing what is broken within us. But what if, instead, we embraced a paradigm shift? What if we recognized the splendor of our garden in its current state, not because it is flawless, but because it is ours – a reflection of our unique journey, experiences, and inherent worth. This recognition doesn't halt our progress but rather enriches our journey towards the life of our dreams with self-love and acceptance.

Consider for a moment the relationship we often have with ourselves. Many of us, including myself, have faced mornings where rising from bed feels like a herculean task. We grapple with making choices that align with our well-being, be it in our diet, exercise, or relationships. It's akin to being in a perpetual tug-of-war with our own essence. We are trapped in this belief that we are perpetually falling short, that a utopian future version of ourselves is the only one worthy of happiness and acceptance.

But let's pause and ponder: what if this constant battle is the result of a flawed tool we've been wielding? A tool akin to an experimental medicine with unforeseen

❖

side effects. We've been conditioned to view ourselves through a lens of inadequacy, always in need of fixing, always a step away from being 'enough'. This mindset, while potentially motivating, can also breed discontentment and self-rejection.

Let's explore an alternative perspective, one where we view ourselves as complete and perfect in this very moment. Imagine loving yourself wholly, embracing every flaw, every scar as a testament to your journey. From this place of unconditional self-love, the desire to improve, to grow, isn't born out of inadequacy but out of a deep-seated love for oneself. It's a recognition that wanting to exercise more, eat healthier, or make better life choices isn't a mission to fix what's broken, but an act of nurturing what we cherish – ourselves.

We stand at a crossroads, with the well-trodden path of self-critique on one side and the less traveled road of self-acceptance on the other. If the former path has left us feeling unfulfilled, why not venture down the new path? What might unfold if we embraced ourselves wholly, with all our perceived imperfections?

This journey of self-acceptance is not a passive one. It is an active, dynamic process of continually acknowledging and appreciating who we are at this moment. It's about finding joy in the 'now', understanding that happiness is not a destination in the future, but a state of being we can access right now.

Your Story

Echoes of the Heart:
Unraveling the Imago Enigma

We often find ourselves entangled in the intricate web of relationships. This journey, rich in its complexity, sometimes becomes a maze where every turn seems hauntingly familiar, echoing past encounters and emotions. It was in this labyrinth that I found myself, perpetually encountering shadows of the same relationship, regardless of the different faces and places. Each relationship, though blooming like a vibrant flower, would inevitably wither into a familiar pattern of neglect, misunderstanding, and unfulfilled promises. In this cycle of repetition, I stood at a crossroads, weary and seeking answers.

It was in this moment of profound questioning that I stumbled upon a beacon of understanding, a concept that would illuminate my path and change my perception of relationships forever - the theory of Imago Therapy. Rooted in the Latin word "imago", meaning "An unconscious idealized mental image of someone, especially a parent, which influences a person's behavior.", this concept unravels the enigmatic pattern of our adult relationships being subtly shaped by our early childhood experiences. Pioneered by Dr. Harville Hendrix and Dr. Helen LaKelly Hunt in 1980, Imago Relationship Therapy is not just a therapeutic approach, but a journey towards self-discovery and healing, turning conflicts into stepping stones for growth and deeper connection.

❖

Imagine a child, whose innocence and vulnerability are met with criticism or neglect. These early scars etch deep into their psyche, resurfacing later in life within the realms of their most intimate relationships. The criticism they once endured now becomes a hypersensitive trigger in the presence of a partner. The abandonment and neglect, once a shadow in their childhood, now loom over their adult commitments. This intricate dance of past and present forms the crux of our relational challenges.

Imago Therapy offers a lens to view these "core issues" not as mere relationship hurdles but as portals to understanding and empathizing with our deepest "childhood wounds". It's a journey towards a "Conscious Relationship", where healing is mutual, and growth is shared. It beckons us to see our partners not as adversaries but as allies in healing our deepest, often unacknowledged, wounds.

The revelation that struck me most profoundly was the realization that my struggles were not just with my partner, but with my own imago – a complex construct shaped by my early caregivers. This imago, born from every unmet need, fear, and pain of my childhood, became a blueprint of my relational expectations. We all, in our own ways, respond to these unmet needs, either through overt expressions like incessant crying or through inward retreat, denying our own needs. As we grow, society molds us further, teaching us what is acceptable and lovable, and in this process, we often lose touch with parts of our true selves.

Your Story

The Feast of Emptiness: A Journey Beyond the Illusion of Fullness

As you delve into these pages, remember, it's not just a narrative; it's a mirror reflecting your inner self, prompting you to question who you truly are.

Imagine standing at the crossroads of transformation, where every direction leads to a different version of yourself. It was at such a junction that I found myself, weighed down by 270 pounds of not just physical weight, but the burden of years of overindulgence and neglect. Peering at my reflection, I was a stranger to myself, a culmination of unrecognizable choices and habits. This physical manifestation was but a shadow of a deeper turmoil, marred by anger, sadness, depression, and a sense of brokenness. It was a wake-up call, a moment of reckoning that spurred a decision to change, to curate new habits to mend not just my body, but my soul.

The core of my transformational journey was not the food itself, but what it represented in my life. It was my greatest addiction, the sun around which every aspect of my existence orbited. From the first thought at dawn to the last whisper at night, food was my constant companion, my silent ruler. Yet, in this incessant focus, I had become blind to its chokehold on my beliefs, my life. And so, fasting entered my life, first as a liberator and then, paradoxically, as a captor.

Embarking on this path, I engaged in light fasting, initially making small strides.

❖

But it was not until my first week-long fast that I experienced a seismic shift. This fast was transcendental, an out-of-body experience that felt like a brush with enlightenment. On the third day, a wave of bliss washed over me, a state of being that lasted for the remainder of the fast. It was a glimpse of an unknown realm of existence, a place of peace and clarity that I yearned to return to.

Eager to recapture this euphoria, I embarked on regular fasting, every three months. Each fast was a quest to return to that blissful state. However, by my fourth fast, a troubling realization dawned upon me. The magic of the first experience eluded me. In my eagerness to replicate that moment of enlightenment, I had unwittingly fallen into the same trap I had with food. I had become fixated on fasting as the key to awareness, losing sight of the fact that it was merely a vehicle, not the destination.

This revelation led me to a deeper understanding of tradition and belief. We often cling to traditions as a means to an end, believing they will lead us to enlightenment. But in doing so, we lose the essence of awareness, which lies not in the pursuit of a preconceived outcome but in embracing the journey itself, in letting things be as they are.

Before I embarked on this journey, depression was my shadow. Post-enlightenment, it remains a part of me. Fasting revealed a path I had never known, but in my fixation on the process, I lost its true gift. It's crucial to understand that the key to self-awareness lies beyond the trappings of our rituals and routines. As you journey through life, ponder this: What are your rituals and traditions? Are they paths to self-discovery, or are they veils that obscure your true self? The feast of emptiness is not about starvation of the body, but about filling the soul with the richness of self-awareness and acceptance. It's a journey beyond the illusion of fullness, into the realm of true understanding and peace.

Remember that the true awakening lies not in the rituals we adopt, but in the moments of clarity they might bring. The feast of emptiness is not a call to deprive oneself but to nourish the soul with introspection and understanding. May you find your path in these words, and may they guide you to a place of true self-awareness and peace.

Your Story

From Life's Shadows to Light: Breaking the Cycles of Existential Echoes

In a world incessantly buzzing with the noise of endless cycles - birth, life, pain, and the elusive chase of happiness - a friend recently approached me with a profound question that echoes the depths of human yearning. He asked, 'How can I break free from the cycle of reincarnation completely? I desire no more lives. I long to be finished.' This wasn't a simple query about escaping physical existence; it was a deeper plea for liberation from the intangible chains of pain, loneliness, struggle, and the relentless tides of emotional poverty. He yearned for his soul's lessons to be learned once and for all, yearning for a state of being rather than becoming, a realm where existence isn't a burden but a symphony of peace.

I am going to attempt to gift you freedom. But understand, this freedom is not mine to give; it's already within you. These words are mere reflections, echoes of the truth residing in your heart. If they stir emotions within you - be it anger, sadness, joy, or enlightenment - know that it was always you who held the key to your chains and your liberation.

Our journey through life is often clouded by our perceptions of pain and suffering. Pain, in its intricate complexity, is subjective. There's no universal scale to measure its intensity or impact. It varies as much as our fingerprints. Some find a strange solace in pain, a kind of masochistic pleasure. Even in medical science, when patients were asked to rate their pain while on medication like Oxycontin, their responses were deeply personal, shaped by their mental and emotional framework.

Consider this: the level of pain we endure is proportional to our resistance to the situation at hand. More often than not, emotional pain is rooted in fear. When we lose a loved one, the heart-wrenching sadness isn't just about loss; it's the fear of never experiencing that unique love again. When we explode in anger or dissolve into tears due to mistreatment, it's not just the act that hurts us; it's the fear of being misunderstood, the fear that our perspectives will remain unseen.

Every emotional turmoil – be it frustration, despair, anxiety, shame, disappointment, loneliness, jealousy, contempt, guilt, bitterness – is steeped in fear. One might argue that this viewpoint comes from a place of privilege. Indeed, I acknowledge my privilege, but this understanding is born from immersing myself in the stories of those who faced the darkest corners of human existence. Books like 'The Gulag Archipelago' and 'Man's Search for Meaning' provide powerful testimonies. People who lost everything found solace and strength in their beliefs, in their inner world, which remained unconquered even when their physical world was in ruins.

Viktor Frankl, a beacon of wisdom, said, 'Man does not simply exist but always decides what his existence will be, what he will become the next moment. By the same token, every human being has the freedom to change at any instant.' Reflect on this: what aspects of our culture have instilled in you the belief that life is a series of lessons to be learned, a ladder of suffering to be climbed? Who whispered these half-truths into the sanctum of your beliefs?

It is not the external situations or actions of others that carve the depths of our suffering; it is our interpretation, our internal dialogue about these events that crafts our pain. Eckhart Tolle, in his enlightening work 'The Power of Now', states, "Don't look for peace. Don't look for any other state than the one you are in now; otherwise, you will set up inner conflict and unconscious resistance. Forgive yourself for not being at peace. The moment you completely accept your non-peace, your non-peace becomes transmuted into peace. Anything you accept fully will get you there, will take you into peace. This is the miracle of surrender." (Tolle) Our quest for peace often becomes a mirage when we focus too much on the past and the future, ignoring the power of now, the only moment we truly own.

In our relentless pursuit of tranquility, we overlook the beauty of the present moment. We falsely believe that our current suffering is a result of past mistakes or future anxieties, but this is an illusion. The root of all suffering and the key to all freedom lies within you. You are a boundless being, experiencing the vastness of life.

I often liken life to my favorite movies. The best ones take you through a rollercoaster of emotions. They make you cry, laugh, and feel every shade of human experience. You empathize with the characters, feel their joy, their pain, their triumphs. But when the movie ends, you don't carry those emotions with you. You leave the theater with gratitude, having had the chance to experience such a rich tapestry of feelings. Live your life like that – embrace the full spectrum of emotions, and always find that space in your heart that is grateful for the experience of life in this very moment.

You, my friend, are a manifestation of the universe, a perfect embodiment of this moment. The universe is within you, and you are within the universe. I see you, asleep in the dream of suffering, of reincarnation, of endless seeking. It's time to awaken to the truth of your existence, to the peace that's been within you all along. Embrace the journey, for it is in this very journey that freedom lies. The path isn't about escaping life, but about embracing it, about understanding that the chains we feel are often of our own making. Break free, not by seeking an end to life, but by understanding the depth and beauty of life itself. Remember, you are the universe experiencing itself, and in this realization, lies your freedom.

Your Story

Unconditional Loves Morality:
A Lost Society Cry For Help

In the bustling avenues of our Western culture, we're deeply entangled in a web of moral codes, a labyrinth that often leads us to question the essence of our existence. But have you ever paused and pondered, "Does it have to be this way?" Imagine a world stripped of laws and consequences. Would humanity spiral into chaos, or is this fear a reflection of our cultural fabric, woven with threads of separation and a relentless quest for more?

Reflecting on the profound words of Alan Watts, who eloquently said, "Money simply represents wealth in the same way that the menu represents dinner," we're led to a crucial realization. We live in a society hypnotized by the illusion of wealth, mistaking the menu for the meal. But what happens when a culture, including its spirituality, becomes so fixated on materiality that it loses sight of true wealth?

In this world, we feel disconnected. Our strength, we're led to believe, springs from the ego, the resounding "I AM." Those with less may feel justified in taking from those with more, driven by a philosophy of 'by any means necessary.' It's a world where morality becomes a necessity, not because it's inherent to our nature, but because we've been taught to divide our love between those we care for and those we don't. And in this division, we lose sight of what it means to love unconditionally.

Consider the wise words of Humble The Poet from his enlightening book "How To Be Love(d)": "Receiving unconditional love is a pipe dream; accessing it, on the other hand, is completely possible." (Poet) This profound statement unveils a truth we often overlook. As a culture obsessed with receiving, we've neglected the eternal essence of love. We cannot control whether we receive love from others, be it parents, lovers, or children. Yet, no one can strip us of our inherent capacity to love unconditionally. By embracing this form of love, we unlock a path to loving ourselves in ways we've rarely experienced in our Western paradigm.

Now, envision a world where, instead of obsessively seeking love from external sources, we turn that immense capacity inward. We nurture a self-love that's free of conditions, a love so profound that it renders external validation irrelevant. In this space, gratitude for the sheer wonder of existence becomes unshakeable. Such a world transcends the need for morals, for why would we ever treat another in a way that leads to negativity or pain? The cost would be too great, not in material terms, but in the currency of emotional and spiritual well-being.

As we embark on this journey of self-discovery and unconditional love, let us remember that the moral compass we so diligently seek to guide us is already within us. It's embedded in our ability to love without limits, to see beyond the illusions of material wealth, and to recognize the interconnectedness of all beings.

In this transformative process, we're not just redefining morality; we're redefining ourselves. We're moving from a culture of acquisition to one of appreciation, from a mindset of scarcity to one of abundance in love and compassion. This shift isn't just about changing how we interact with others; it's about transforming how we view ourselves and our place in the universe.

So, as we navigate the complexities of life, let's challenge ourselves to look beyond the superficial. Let's strive to understand the deeper currents that shape our thoughts, actions, and relationships. By doing so, we not only elevate our own existence but also contribute to a more loving, compassionate, and morally grounded world.

Remember, the journey to unconditional love and a higher moral understanding begins not outside, but within. It starts with a simple yet profound shift in perspective, a commitment to exploring the depths of our own hearts and minds. As we embark on this path, let's embrace each step with curiosity, compassion, and an unwavering belief in the transformative power of love.

In closing, I invite you to awaken to the possibilities that lie within you. Embrace the journey with an open heart and mind, and discover the boundless potential of a life lived in harmony with love and morality. Let's not just dream of a better world; let's be the architects of it, one act of unconditional love at a time. I hope you wake up.

Your Story

Losing god To Find God

In the quiet moments of introspection, where the mind's chatter subsides and the heart begins to speak, I came across a thought that lingered in the depths of my consciousness: "Maybe your belief about god is what keeps you from God." This simple yet profound idea struck a chord within me, challenging my long-held perceptions of the divine.

Growing up in the church's embrace, I was surrounded by teachings and doctrines that painted a picture of God – a canvas of expectations, rules, and interpretations. Despite my earnest efforts to connect, a nagging feeling of disconnect persisted. Like an actor on a stage, I played my part, concealing my doubts and fears, ever so afraid of being unmasked for feeling differently.

Why, I wondered, did I feel so distant from what others seemed to embrace so effortlessly? Was my inability to feel what they felt a reflection of my own spiritual inadequacy? These questions haunted me, casting a shadow on my spiritual journey.

Then, one day, a statement echoed in my mind, altering my perspective: "If God is all-powerful and all-knowing, what does God lack?" The answer was simple yet revolutionary: "Limits." This concept of an omnipotent God, boundless and infinite, led me to question the paradox of our human tendency to ascribe limitations to the divine. Do we, in our limited understanding, inadvertently assume the power to disrupt God's grand plan?

I do not claim to have all the answers, but this revelation shed light on the limitations of language in comprehending the divine. Language, by its very nature, categorizes and defines, setting boundaries on what is and isn't. Yet, how can we define the indefinable? If God exists, God simply 'is' – beyond the confines of human language and understanding.

For years, my concept of God was shrouded in attributes of vengeance, anger, and disappointment. It never occurred to me to question why an omnipotent being would experience such human emotions. Isn't everything, including our perceived flaws and mistakes, part of a larger, incomprehensible divine plan? In dissecting the whole into manageable pieces, we lose sight of the grandeur and interconnectedness of existence.

The realization that the perceived separation between us and God is an illusion brings a profound sense of peace. How can we, mere fragments of the universe, be separate from the whole? The omnipotence of the divine stretches to every corner of existence, even to the places our minds cannot fathom. Our inability to fully understand does not diminish the vastness of the divine narrative.

Language, in its attempt to describe the indescribable, falls short. It is said that the language of God is silence, and everything else is a mistranslation. This enigmatic statement invites us to explore the divine not through words, but through the stillness and quietude of our being. What then, does this mean for the 'Word of God'? How do we reconcile the profoundness of silence with the teachings and scriptures that have guided us for centuries?

In this exploration, I have come to understand that the divine cannot be confined to pages, sermons, or doctrines. It is an experience, a feeling, a knowing that transcends the limitations of human expression. It is in the moments of deep meditation, in the acts of unconditional love, and in the beauty of the natural world that we catch glimpses of the divine.

As I reflect on this journey, I am reminded of the words of the mystic poet Rumi: "The quieter you become, the more you are able to hear." (Rumi) In the stillness of our hearts and minds, we open ourselves to the possibility of experiencing the divine in its purest form – unfiltered, unbounded, and utterly ineffable.

My hope for you is that you awaken to the divine presence that permeates every aspect of your life. May you find the courage to let go of limiting beliefs and open your heart to the limitless love and wisdom of the universe. In doing so, you will discover that you are not separate from the divine; you are a beautiful, integral part of it.

Remember, the journey to understanding the divine is not about seeking answers outside of yourself; it is about turning inward and discovering the truth that has always resided within you. It is a journey of unlearning, of shedding layers of conditioned beliefs, and of embracing the mystery and majesty of existence.

As you embark on this path, be gentle with yourself. Allow your understanding to evolve, your heart to expand, and your spirit to soar. In the words of Lao Tzu, "The journey of a thousand miles begins with a single step." Take that step with an open heart, and let the journey transform you.

Your Story

Embracing the Full Spectrum
of Holiday Emotions

The holiday season, a mosaic of emotions and memories, unfolds differently in the hearts of each individual. For many, it's a time of warmth, a celebration of love and togetherness. For others, it stands as a poignant reminder of what's missing – a love lost or perhaps a love that never was. It's a period that can simultaneously cradle us in joy and confront us with the depths of our own vulnerabilities.

Reflecting on this duality, I'm reminded of a profound truth from the "Tao of Fully Feeling": "The only pain that can be avoided is the pain that comes from trying to avoid unavoidable pain... Time does not heal wounds without acknowledgement of what has happened." In these words lies the essence of life's most challenging lessons. To live is to experience, to feel – both the highs and the lows. Today, for me, is one of those days marked by a sense of loss, a reminder of the transient nature of all things.

Life, in its purest form, is akin to a cinematic masterpiece, filled with scenes that make our hearts soar and others that shatter them into a million pieces. Today, I embrace my losses, not with attachment, but with a deep involvement that life demands. Enlightenment doesn't immunize us against pain. Before my journey towards enlightenment, I experienced depression. Now, as an enlightened soul, the shadow of depression still lurks. But herein lies a profound realization: the beliefs and experiences that bring us joy also have the power to introduce us to its antithesis – the pain of loss, the sting of hurt.

Yet, I do not suffer. I am bathed in gratitude for the myriad of opportunities that have graced my life over the past 31 years. I don't languish in despair over moments taken for granted; instead, I see them as valuable lessons. The memories of those no longer with us are cherished, a testament to being fully present in the time we had together.

My own experiences have forged a path of deeper understanding and empathy for others in their moments of pain and suffering. To them, I offer the wise words from a sermon of A.W. Tozer: "It is doubtful whether God can bless a man greatly until He has hurt him deeply." To feel the depth of your current emotions is to acknowledge that you've loved deeply and completely. What greater experience is there in life than to have loved with all your heart?

In the spirit of healing and forgiveness, I reflect upon another passage from the "Tao of Fully Feeling": "I pray that I may be graced with the cleansing waters of forgiveness... Let me learn to forgive others by becoming more forgiving of myself." (Walker) Forgiveness, a journey of the soul, begins within and radiates outward. It's a path that teaches us to differentiate between those we need to forgive and stay close to, those we need to forgive and keep a distance from, and those whom forgiveness isn't necessary.

Tonight, I choose to immerse myself fully in the spectrum of emotions that life offers. I embrace the life I have been blessed with, filled with gratitude for the time shared and the love given and received. Until the end of my days, I will continue to love unconditionally. I am thankful for the fragments of my soul that I've discovered and pieced together through these experiences.

As the holiday season unfolds, let us remember that it's not just a time for celebration but also a period for reflection, healing, and growth. It's an opportunity to delve deep into our hearts, to confront our emotions, and to emerge stronger and more connected to ourselves and others. Let's cherish each moment, whether it fills us with joy or brings us to tears, for each experience is a step on the path to wisdom and enlightenment.

In closing, remember that life, in all its complexity, is a beautiful journey. The holidays are but a microcosm of this journey, encapsulating love, loss, joy, and pain. Embrace it all, for in doing so, you embrace the fullness of being.

I hope you wake up...

Your Story

The Endless Vacation: Weaving a Life Beyond the Need for Escapes

Where would you vacation if there was nothing to vacation from?

In the tapestry of modern Western culture, there's a peculiar fascination with the concept of vacation - a magical time when we step away from the madness of daily life to bask in the freedom and leisure we yearn for. But let's pause and reflect: what if we could cultivate a life from which there's nothing to escape? What if every day could be imbued with the essence of that dreamed vacation?

Vacation, by its traditional definition, is an extended period of leisure and recreation, often spent traveling or away from home. Yet, at its core, it represents something deeper - an escape from the ordinary, a temporary release from the routines that bind us. For many, life feels compartmentalized into phases of enduring and escaping. We work, we strive, we endure, all in anticipation of those fleeting moments of escape. But let's envision a different narrative - a life so fulfilling, so aligned with our deepest passions, that the line between living and vacationing blurs.

Often, when we reflect on our vacations, there's a tinge of dissatisfaction - it wasn't long enough, the dread of returning, the immediate planning of the next escape. This cycle begs the question: Are we ever truly present? Even in these moments of supposed freedom, are we truly free if our minds are shackled to the thought of what comes next?

But who taught us that life had to be a series of endurance and escape? Do we even remember who first introduced us to the concept of a vacation? These ingrained beliefs, often unexamined, shape our perception of life. But imagine, if offered the chance to step into a life that no longer requires these escapes, would we dare to take it?

Imagine the perfect vacation, one where you never have to return to the mundane. At first, it seems idyllic - endless days by the beach, a drink in hand, the sun kissing your skin. But soon, a realization dawns: the allure of the beach and the drinks was not in their essence, but in their role as an escape. What happens when there's nothing to escape from? Does the sweetness of escape fade when it becomes the norm?

Often, we don't recall where our beliefs and ideas originated, making it challenging to question them. Yet, this process of unlearning and relearning is vital. If I could gift you a life that never needed another vacation, a life where every day is a celebration of your true self, would you embrace it?

Crafting a life that feels like a continuous vacation doesn't mean abandoning responsibilities or work. It means aligning our daily lives with our passions, finding joy in the mundane, and seeing each day as an opportunity for growth and happiness. This alignment brings about a life where the need for escape diminishes because the life we live is the life we love.

In essence, this journey is about crafting a life that doesn't necessitate an escape. It's about finding that paradise not in distant lands but within ourselves and our daily experiences. This life, a life where every day is as enriching as a vacation, is not just a possibility but a choice we can make. It's about redefining what life means to us, breaking free from the conventional, and embracing the beauty of the present.

A life beyond the need for vacations is a life full of purpose, passion, and joy. It's a life where we are not constantly looking forward to escaping but are deeply immersed in the beauty of the now. This, perhaps, is the greatest journey we can undertake - a journey not to new destinations, but to a new way of experiencing life itself.

Your Story

Comet of Time:
Illuminating the Journey of Now

What kind of life will you gift your time?

In the whirlwind of life, especially during the festive season, our minds often wander towards the future. We find ourselves eagerly anticipating the joys to come, or perhaps anxiously dreading the end of a vacation. In these moments, caught in the currents of time, we tend to overlook the beauty of now. This phenomenon, a common thread in the tapestry of human experience, reveals a profound truth about our existence: the paradox of living in the moment while being swept away by the tides of time.

Think about it. When you're having a great time, they say time flies. But have you ever wondered why? Perhaps it's because a truly good life, filled with meaningful experiences, is like a comet streaking across the sky – brilliant, breathtaking, but all too brief. Reflect on your childhood. Remember how you were always taught to look forward? To summer breaks, graduations, the first day of high school, the excitement of college, the thrill of your first job, the anticipation of your birthday, the joy of Christmas. It seems like our lives are structured as a series of forward-looking milestones. But in this constant forward motion, when do we pause to savor the present?

For the majority of my life, I too was always looking ahead, thrilled by the promise of what was yet to come. And yet, in this forward gaze, I realized I was missing the beauty of my current experiences. It's only when we reach these milestones that we often look back with nostalgia, wishing to relive those moments, recognizing their value only in retrospect. Western culture, with its relentless pace and endless distractions, rarely encourages us to stop and appreciate the now. We're always in pursuit of the next big thing, aren't we?

But let me ask you this: Do you truly know what you love most in this life? Or are you fixated on the dissatisfaction of your current circumstances? I had to confront a hard truth – my unhappiness stemmed not from my circumstances, but from my inability to appreciate where I was. I remember thinking, "If only I could skip to the good parts of life, everything would be perfect." Whether it was longing for my first job, dreaming of my first apartment, or yearning for any number of firsts, I was perpetually living in the future, blind to the joys of the present.

Consider this profound thought: We are but a speck in the vast expanse of the universe. Even those fortunate to live a century barely register a blip on the timeline of existence. This realization should not evoke despair, but rather a sense of urgency – an urgency to cherish every moment we have. Love the people in your life deeply and without reservation. Ask yourself, What kind of life do I want to gift my time? And live it."

As we navigate the holidays and beyond, let's try to shift our focus. Let's not just capture moments through lenses or social media posts, but truly experience them with our hearts. Let's be present for our loved ones, for the laughter, the conversations, the warmth of shared experiences. These moments, fleeting as they may be, are where true joy lies.

In this journey of life, let us remember that every moment is a gift – a unique, irreplaceable opportunity to create, to love, to live. So, embrace the now with open arms and an open heart. For in doing so, you're not just passing through time; you're making every second count.

Your Story

Dancing Souls: The Art of Sharing Wholeness in Togetherness

In the end, love is not just about finding the right person. It's about being the right person.

From the earliest whispers of our childhood, we are fed tales and expectations about love that shape our pursuit of this elusive emotion. We are told that finding love and nurturing it is akin to embarking on an epic journey – the most difficult yet fulfilling quest of our lives.

In my conversations with countless souls, a recurring theme surfaces – no one claims that the path of marriage or partnership is free from trials. This sentiment echoes loudly in the Western world, where marriage and parenthood are viewed as pinnacle life experiences, simultaneously the most challenging and rewarding. But, let's pause and ponder: What if this perception is a self-fulfilling prophecy? What if, in expecting hardships, we inadvertently weave them into the fabric of our relationships?

I firmly believe in the power of cultural narratives to shape our realities. Consider a child, nurtured on the belief that love and marriage are arduous journeys, destined to be the most fulfilling aspects of human existence. Such a child might grow into an adult who unconsciously seeks out struggles in relationships, validating the ingrained belief. Alternatively, this child may choose a different path, yet be constantly reminded by society that they are missing out on life's supposed greatest fulfillment.

But what happens when these narratives are juxtaposed with the fairy-tale ideal – the belief in a magical, effortless love where everything aligns perfectly? This dichotomy sets the stage for a profound internal conflict: the expectation of ease and challenge, leading to a tumultuous journey through love, constantly seeking validation to feel complete.

Could this paradox be a contributing factor to the high rates of relationship failures we observe? Does it drive the endless quest for validation through relationships, even as previous ones crumble? It's time for a cultural reawakening – a realization that breaking free from this cycle of suffering begins with self-love.

Envision a world where individuals enter relationships not out of need, but from a place of wholeness. Where love is not about filling a void within ourselves but about sharing our completeness with another. In this paradigm, love is not a crutch but a dance – a space where two souls, secure in their own beings, come together to grow, not out of necessity, but out of choice.

This form of love is rooted in openness, transparency, and vulnerability. It's about loving someone for who they are, not for what they bring to your life. It's about giving them the freedom to be their true selves, as you both evolve together. This is not a utopian fantasy; it's the gift of awareness. It's the understanding that true love is not about possession or fear of loss, but about mutual growth and respect.

So, I pose a question to you: Does our culture truly understand love? Have we been so entangled in the narratives handed down to us that we've lost sight of love's true essence? It's time to redefine love, not as a quest laden with predetermined struggles but as a journey of self-discovery, where finding love in another is a natural extension of the love we cultivate within ourselves.

In this reimagined narrative, love is not a destination but a journey – a continuous process of learning, understanding, and growing. It's about unlearning the myths and relearning the truths. It's about stepping away from societal scripts and writing our own stories of love, grounded in authenticity and self-awareness.

As we embark on this transformative journey, let us remember that the love we seek is a reflection of the love we nurture within ourselves. Let's embrace love not as a societal mandate, but as a personal journey of growth and fulfillment. In doing so, we might just uncover the true essence of love, free from the chains of cultural expectations and rich in the beauty of genuine connection.

In the end, love is not just about finding the right person. It's about being the right person. It's about evolving and growing into someone who can love deeply, authentically, and unconditionally. And in this journey of personal transformation, we might just find that the love we seek has been within us all along

Your Story

Embracing the Journey Beyond Suffering: A Path to Overcoming Narcissism

Consider this: often, we cling to our pain because it is the last link to something or someone we have lost. It's a bittersweet reminder of what was once a part of us

In our lives, we often encounter moments of pain and suffering that feel insurmountable. This pain, though deeply wounding, can paradoxically become a defining part of our identity. As I have explored in my own journey and in the countless stories I've encountered, there is a profound truth hidden in these experiences: sometimes, the path to healing is not just about moving away from pain, but also about understanding its role in our lives.

Consider this: often, we cling to our pain because it is the last link to something or someone we have lost. It's a bittersweet reminder of what was once a part of us. This clinging, while it may seem counterintuitive, is a deeply human response. Our pain becomes a lens through which we view the world, shaping our interactions, our choices, and even our dreams.

But there's a deeper layer to this attachment to pain. It's not just about holding onto the past; it's about fearing the unknown future. "Who am I without my pain and suffering?" This question haunted me for years. I realized that outside of my pain, I was unsure of my identity. I was aware of my surface-level traits – my sense of humor, my job – but none of these felt as real or as defining as the pain I had endured.

As we journey through life, unhealed wounds can create a repetitive cycle. We find ourselves drawn to similar relationships, facing analogous challenges at work, and engaging in familiar conflicts. It's as though life is trying to teach us a lesson that we haven't quite grasped yet. In my experience, this repetition was not just a coincidence; it was a reflection of the lessons I needed to learn.

However, there's a risk in this cycle. Holding onto pain can inadvertently lead us to inflict similar pain on others. It's not out of malice, but out of a human desire to not feel alone in our suffering. In my case, this manifested in ways I wasn't proud of. I became self-centered, not in an overtly arrogant way, but in a way where my pain took center stage in every interaction. I realized that I had become what I feared the most – a person who, in the throes of unaddressed pain, had begun to hurt those I cared about the most.

This brings us to a critical point in our journey: the moment of awakening. For me, it was a startling realization that I had been living as a narcissist. This term often conjures images of grandiose self-importance, but at its core, narcissism can be a defense mechanism against deep-seated pain and a lack of self-esteem. It's a way of seeking constant validation and placing oneself at the center of the universe to avoid confronting inner wounds.

In this self-centered universe, genuine connections become impossible. We're so focused on maintaining our world that we fail to see how we're impacting others. For me, this realization was a turning point. It was the moment I recognized the need to let go of the identity I had clung to – an identity built around my pain and suffering.

The journey beyond pain is not just about healing; it's about transformation. It's about asking ourselves, "Who can I become when I am not defined by my suffering?" This question is not easy to answer. It requires a deep dive into the unknown parts of ourselves, the parts we've neglected or hidden away.

In my journey, I learned that healing was not just about erasing the pain but about understanding its role in my life. It was about learning to see pain as a teacher, not just a tormentor. This shift in perspective is not a denial of pain but an acknowledgment of its power to transform us.

As we embrace this journey, we open ourselves to new possibilities. We learn to forge connections that are rooted in authenticity and vulnerability. We discover that our greatest strengths often arise from our deepest wounds. And perhaps most importantly, we learn that our pain, once a source of suffering, can become a catalyst for profound personal growth and a deeper understanding of the human experience.

In closing, I invite you to reflect on your own relationship with pain. Is it holding you back, or is it guiding you toward a deeper understanding of yourself? Remember, the journey of healing is not just about moving away from pain but also about moving towards a greater sense of self-awareness and purpose.

As you walk this path, know that you are not alone. Each step you take is a step towards a more authentic, more compassionate, and more fulfilled version of yourself. Embrace the journey, for it is in traversing these challenging paths that we discover our true potential and the boundless possibilities that life offers.

Your Story

Who Are You Liberating Yourself From?
A Journey to Self-Understanding

The struggles I faced were often those projected onto me by others. We're taught that life is a struggle, but what if we never needed to accept this narrative?

"Who are you liberating yourself from?" This question isn't just a query; it's an invitation to embark on the most significant journey you'll ever undertake – the journey within.

We grow up in a world that's full of invisible traps. These traps, often cloaked in good intentions, convince us to act against our best interests. But have you ever paused to consider who sets these traps? Is our suffering the result of others' actions, or is it born from our perceptions of these actions?

Let me share a personal reflection. As a young boy, I was taught how to perceive people's actions – what was respectful, what was considered loving, and what was narcissistic. But how often do we conclude someone's intentions not based on what they actually say, but on what we think they mean? How can we ever truly know if someone loves us, or if they are genuinely our best friend? What do these labels even mean? What I failed to understand initially was that my perception of their actions actually mirrored how I saw and accepted myself. The tension I experienced in our interactions was frequently a manifestation of the internal conflicts I was grappling with.

Throughout my life, I've faced numerous struggles. In those moments, it felt as if life was unraveling. Yet, looking back, I see a different picture. I see life stitching itself together, creating a tapestry that was meant just for me. Were my frustrations born from unmet expectations, or were they a natural reaction to the challenges of the moment?

In our quest for personal development, we're often led to believe that we need 'fixing.' That if we just follow the right process, we can morph into our ideal selves. I, too, believed this. But then I asked myself, "Who am I really changing?" If I am trying to fix myself, who is the 'I' doing the fixing? It's like peeling an onion – layer by layer, until nothing is left. Were those layers ever really separate from the core?

This brings us to the eternal battle of good versus evil within us. We fracture our identity, believing that one part of us must be defeated for another to thrive. But what if all these parts are inherently us? What if this fragmentation is a result of the narratives we've been fed, rather than our true nature?

I recall the internal battles I faced just to get out of bed and go to the gym. Part of me yearned for self-improvement, while another part just wanted to rest and savor the moment. Who was the real 'me' in this scenario? There was a part of me that regretted past choices, another that accepted life's outcomes, a side that was anxious and stressed, and yet another that found joy in simple pleasures.

This journey led me to a powerful realization about self-fulfilling prophecies. The struggles I faced were often those projected onto me by others. We're taught that life is a struggle, but what if we never needed to accept this narrative? What if the friction we feel with reality is simply a clash between our beliefs and our experiences?

Right now, as you read these words, consider this moment. Yes, there might be problems ahead, and yes, there may have been mistakes in the past. But what if, just for now, this moment is perfect as it is?

In essence, the path to self-liberation is not about escaping from something or someone. It's about rediscovering and embracing every part of ourselves – understanding that each emotion, each thought, and each experience is a vital piece of the puzzle that makes us who we are. It's about learning to view our journey through a lens of compassion and mindfulness, recognizing that every step, whether it feels like a stumble or a stride, is a part of our unique, beautiful dance of life.

So, I invite you to ask yourself again: "Who are you liberating yourself from?" Maybe, just maybe, the person you're liberating is closer than you think. Could it be you? Waiting to be understood, accepted, and loved for all that you are.

Your Story

The Illusion of Loneliness:
A Journey To Genuine Connection

In western culture it's easy to mistake being physically alone for loneliness. But these two states are as distinct as night and day. For a significant portion of my life, I grappled with a profound sense of loneliness, a feeling that persistently gnawed at my soul, irrespective of whether I was surrounded by a sea of faces or in the quiet solitude of my room. This experience led me to a revelation: true connection begins not with others, but within ourselves.

In Western culture, where the buzz of life never seems to quiet, we often find ourselves lost in a labyrinth of roles and identities. Consumerism, the very heartbeat of this culture, whispers a subtle yet pervasive message: "You are what you possess." This notion transcends the material and seeps into our sense of self. We identify as mothers, fathers, siblings, lovers, playing roles that we believe define us. But beneath these labels lies a paradoxical question we seldom dare to ask: "Who am I, really?"

Think about this: if every familiar aspect of your life vanished overnight, who would you be? If the world forgot your name, how would that shape your sense of self? If the person you cherish most turned their back on you, how would you find your footing again? I've realized that my own loneliness stemmed from a deep-seated fear that my worth was tied to external validations – being humorous, intelligent, or affluent. But if people loved me only for these attributes, was it really me they loved?

Our modern day Shakespeare Drake, has echoed these sentiments, questioning whether love and appreciation are contingent on what we offer, rather than who we are.

"What if I had a CDL

Leavin' outta STL, on the way to ATL in a big 18-wheel

Would your ass still be here?

Would your ass still be here?

Would you love Ed like you love Drake?

Love Fred like you love Drake?

Love Greg like you love Drake?

Love Ced like you love Drake?

Thought you said that you love Drake?

Thought you said that you love Drake?

Thought you said, ayy"

(Drake)

These questions reveal a profound truth: our essence is not static. We are fluid, ever-evolving beings, constantly renewing ourselves. Each encounter with a friend or stranger is not a mere repetition of the past but a unique interaction with a being who is infinite in their possibilities.

In this recognition lies a paradoxical liberation. Imagine reaching a state where your presence in someone's life is not about need but choice – a choice stemming from pure, unconditional love. In such relationships, fears of deceit, abandonment, and inadequacy dissipate. But embracing this means accepting a world without leverage, where love is given freely, without expectations or conditions.

This brings us to the crux of loneliness: it's often rooted in the fear that our 'leverage' in others' lives might slip away. We strive, sometimes desperately, to be enough, not realizing that this fear itself casts a shadow on our self-worth. The paradox is that in believing we need leverage to maintain relationships, we are left wondering if we are ever truly enough for anyone. But here's a liberating truth: you can only accept others to the extent that you accept yourself.

Embark on a journey of self-love. Embrace moments of solitude as opportunities for introspection and discovery. Peel back the layers of your identity and examine the core of your being. Ask yourself, "Who am I beyond my roles, beyond my achievements, beyond my failures?" "Why do I need marriage to feel validated?" "Why do I seek security in relationships?" "Who do I need to feel whole?" In this self-exploration, you will find a love that is unconditional, a love that doesn't rely on leverage or external validation.

As you cultivate this inner sanctuary of self-acceptance and love, you'll notice a transformation. The loneliness that once felt like a constant companion begins to fade, replaced by a sense of completeness and contentment that comes from within. In this space, every relationship becomes a reflection of your inner peace, not a quest for validation.

To be alone is not to be lonely. Loneliness is a state of mind, a product of disconnection from our true selves. When we connect deeply with our inner being, we discover a universe of love and acceptance that never wanes. It's in this discovery that the illusion of loneliness dissolves, and we find ourselves truly connected – not just with others, but with the very essence of life itself.

Your Story

The Limits of God:
The Paradox of Perception

If God is omnipotent, all-knowing, and all-powerful, what then does God lack? Limits... The very essence of God's omnipotence seems to defy the concept of lacking anything. Yet, when we delve deeper into the human experience, a paradox emerges: the lack of limits. To understand this paradox, we must understand that perspective is shaped by limits. The myriad human emotions – pain, sadness, anger, frustration – arise from the uncertain tides of the future and the unmet expectations of the present. Can an omnipotent God, in His boundless existence, truly partake in these human experiences?

Reflecting on this, let's ponder a profound thought. Our beliefs about God might actually be the barriers that keep us from truly connecting with the divine. Anthony De'Mello said, "Perfect love casts out fear. Where there is love there are no demands, no expectations, no dependency." (De Mello) This powerful statement leads us to question: If God embodies perfect love, why would He impose demands or conditions? Wouldn't an omniscient God understand and accept our choices as part of a grander plan?

This brings us to a crucial introspection. Has our attachment to a defined concept of God led us to a deity that mirrors our human traits – omnipotent yet strikingly human? Alan Watts, a visionary in bridging Eastern wisdom with Western thought, observed,

"God is the most obvious thing in the world. He is absolutely self-evident - the simplest, clearest and closest reality of life and consciousness. We are only unaware of him because we are too complicated, for our vision is darkened by the complexity of pride. We seek him beyond the horizon with our noses lifted high in the air, and fail to see that he lies at our very feet. We flatter ourselves in premeditating the long, long journey we are going to take in order to find him, the giddy heights of spiritual progress we are going to scale, and all the time are unaware of the truth that "God is nearer to us than we are to ourselves." We are like birds flying in quest of the air, or men with lighted candles searching through the darkness for fire." (Watts)

In our efforts to understand God, do we get caught up in defining and labeling, rather than experiencing the perfection that is life itself? We search for peace in external sources – in relationships, achievements, and societal validations. Yet, perhaps in this search, we've strayed from a profound truth: peace and God are not distant, but ever-present. As the scripture gently reminds us, "Look at the birds of the air; they do not sow or reap or store away in barns, and yet your heavenly Father feeds them. Are you not much more valuable than they?" In our complex lives, have we overlooked this simple yet profound answer that peace and God are here and now, waiting for us to shed our preconceived notions?

I'm not here to tell you that your spiritual journey is without merit or that your beliefs are misplaced. Rather, I invite you to reflect. If God is the source of your peace, and you find yourself in a moment devoid of peace, what has caused this separation? If God is omnipotent and all-knowing, what indeed does God lack?

Your Story

The Pursuit of Authenticity: Questioning Life's Assumed Priorities

What truly matters in life? This question isn't just a fleeting thought; it's a profound inquiry that shapes our every action, decision, and thought. It's a quest to understand value, purpose, and meaning in a world that is constantly evolving.

As we navigate through our daily lives, we're often caught in a delicate balance between work and leisure, between today's needs and tomorrow's dreams. When I wake up each day, a part of me silently declares that my work holds more significance than my moments of rest. But is this truly the case? If I prioritize leisure, yet work tirelessly to afford a certain lifestyle, aren't I just chasing tomorrow's pleasure at the expense of today's joy?

This conundrum is not unique to me; it's a universal struggle. Many of us are tirelessly working under the belief that one day we will find rest and contentment. We cling to our jobs, our relationships, and our material possessions as if they define our very existence. They become our security blankets, our identities. But in this relentless pursuit, we often lose sight of what brings us true happiness.

The culture we live in, especially in the West, has taught us to seek external security. We dress a certain way, live in houses, and avoid the unknown, all in an effort to fit into a societal mold. But in doing so, are we truly living? When we encounter someone who breaks these norms, our reactions reveal much about our own insecurities. If we are confident and content with our choices, why would the path of another cause us distress?

Throughout life, I've realized that my strongest reactions – be it anger or unwarranted sympathy – surface when I am most unsure about my own choices. It's a mirror reflecting my inner turmoil, a signal that perhaps I am not as aligned with my true self as I thought.

In moments of discontent, when we wish for a different reality, it's crucial to ask ourselves – why? What is inherently wrong with this moment? Our feelings of inferiority or dissatisfaction are often rooted in subjective assumptions. We can't change the objective facts of our lives, but we can alter our subjective interpretations. Value is a relative concept; it only exists in reference to something else. Just because society agrees on the value of something doesn't make it inherently valuable. It's a shared, subjective interpretation.

Every moment up until now has been objectively perfect in its own way. It is our thoughts and perceptions that add a subjective flavor to it. But imagine, for a moment, if you knew nothing of the world's expectations and norms. How liberating, how blissfully content could you be in your pure, unadulterated existence?

In our journey to find what matters most, it's essential to look inward. The external world is fleeting, ever-changing, and often out of our control. But our inner world – our thoughts, our beliefs, our values – is where true transformation can occur. By understanding and aligning with our inner selves, we unlock the potential to live a life that is not just successful by societal standards, but one that is deeply fulfilling and purposeful.

As we embark on this journey of self-discovery, let us remember that the most profound answers often lie within us. They are waiting to be uncovered in the quiet moments of reflection, in the honest conversations with ourselves, and in the courageous steps we take towards living a life true to our inner calling.

The quest to determine what matters most is not just a pursuit of external achievements or societal validation. It's a deeply personal journey of understanding our own values, beliefs, and desires. It's about finding harmony between our inner world and the external realities, and in doing so, crafting a life that resonates with authenticity, purpose, and joy. Let us embrace this journey with an open heart and a curious mind, for it is in this exploration that we find our true selves and the true essence of life.

This new year, I hope you wake up....

Your Story

Embracing Now: The Journey from Preference to Presence

I was once told that we trade our freedom for preference and I have never been able to see the world the same way again.

Reflect on our beginnings. We entered this world devoid of expectations and attachments, free in the truest sense. Our early days were spent savoring life's simplicity and expressing needs without reservation. However, as we matured, society introduced us to the concept of preferences. We were conditioned to believe that these preferences are synonymous with happiness.

But there's a hidden consequence to this conditioning. Our ability to relish each moment gradually shifted to an anticipation of the next, where we could indulge in our preferences. Over time, our affection for these preferences grew, eclipsing our appreciation for anything that didn't align with them.

This shift wasn't limited to external things; it permeated our self-perception. We began to base our happiness on meeting certain standards – a specific appearance, behavior, or material possession. This conditional self-love created a paradigm where failing to meet these standards equated to a lack of happiness. This mindset extended to how we perceived others.

❖

Consider the implications when our happiness relies on others meeting our preferences. What if they change, no longer aligning with our expectations? Our affection for them often hinges on potential rather than reality, failing to appreciate them for who they truly are. Even when we commit to something or someone, it's often done with the hope that it aligns with our future preferences, not for the current joy it brings.

Many of us fixate on a future moment, believing it will bring ultimate fulfillment – be it a milestone anniversary, retirement, or watching grandchildren grow. We may set personal goals, deferring change until a future date, hoping then to achieve our ideal selves.

However, when our hope for a brighter future is tethered to these preferences, we become enamored with an elusive euphoria. We plan, dream, and prepare for what is to come, but paradoxically, we never seem to reach these aspirations. Happiness remains just out of grasp, leading us to wonder if just a little more effort, a little more time, or a little more change in ourselves will lead to contentment. The reality is, unless we embrace and love ourselves as we are now, satisfaction will always be a distant dream. Our fixation is not with the situation or person but with the notion of something better.

Today, I invite you to introspect. Why can't you love yourself unconditionally right now? What do you believe is missing that prevents you from living your dream life?

In my experience, embracing unconditional love has enabled me to value experiences over preferences. I've learned to cherish every moment for what it brings, not for what it could lead to. My commitments are choices made out of desire, not obligation. My pursuit of health and wellbeing stems from a place of self-love, aspiring to fully enjoy life's journey.

We've been conditioned to believe that preference outweighs freedom, lulling us into a dream of a better future. But the truth is, there is no time more precious than the present. It's time to awaken and recognize the perfection of the here and now, waiting to be embraced and celebrated.

This realization invites us to rediscover our inherent freedom, to live a life not dictated by preferences, but enriched by the beauty and spontaneity of each moment. I hope you wake up.

Your Story

The Challenge of Being True to Ourselves in a Judgmental World

Our identity is a complex weave of experiences, perceptions, and the roles we choose or are assigned. The journey to understanding oneself can be an illuminating path, yet it's fraught with the peril of becoming too ensnared in a singular narrative, a single thread in the vastness of who we are.

Think for a moment: What happens when we fixate too much on the identity we've sculpted for ourselves? When our view of others and ourselves is filtered solely through the lens of this crafted persona, do we risk losing sight of the true nature of our existence? The truth is, identity, as we understand it, is an ever-evolving story, not a static definition.

As we navigate through the odyssey of life, we often encounter the enigma of self-perception versus reality. I recall my own journey with a sense of introspection. For a significant portion of my life, I anchored my identity in the belief that I was the quintessential "good guy." And "good guys" always finish last.

However, a deeper reflection reveals a startling revelation: I was the architect of my own problems. My past is littered with instances where I, unbeknownst to myself, inflicted pain upon others. I pushed people away, preemptively guarding against hurt, only to perpetuate the very cycle I feared. My actions, marred by a lack of self-awareness, often bordered on hostility and rudeness. Yet, in those moments, I was oblivious to the role I played, too entangled in the narrative of victimhood.

This self-imposed victim narrative led to the creation of my villain arc — an arc I believed I had to overcome to prove my worth and righteousness. But perhaps, in seeking this vindication, I was merely chasing a tale of my own making, a story I wanted to narrate about myself.

In the words of Don Miguel Ruiz, there's a profound analogy of the human condition in his book "The Four Agreements." He speaks of a planet where everyone suffers from a skin disease, a poignant metaphor for the emotional scars we bear. Imagine a world where the norm is to live with such pain that the mere act of human touch brings agony. This allegory mirrors our emotional wounds — wounds often invisible to the naked eye yet profoundly impactful in shaping our interactions and relationships.

Ruiz's insights resonate deeply with me, particularly his thoughts on how these emotional wounds, laden with fear, anger, hate, sadness, envy, and hypocrisy, shape our existence. We live in a world where emotional pain has become so normalized that it's often mistaken for the status quo, thereby perpetuating a cycle of suffering.

This understanding has led me to a crucial realization about my own life. The suffering I endure is often a reflection of how I treat myself. It's a mirror showing me how my actions and thoughts reverberate through my interactions with others. Recognizing this, I've embarked on a journey to shed the self-imposed titles and narratives that have long defined me. I've begun to unravel the threads of my identity, seeking to understand rather than judge, to heal rather than harm.

In seeking peace, I've learned to question the narratives I've clung to. Is the suffering I experience necessary for my growth, or is it a chain I've forged through my perceptions and actions? In asking these questions, I invite anyone grappling with similar struggles to ponder their paths. How can we wake up from the self-created dreams of suffering? Is it possible that what we seek lies not in proving ourselves to others but in finding peace within?

As we embark on this journey of self-discovery and healing, I encourage exploring the wisdom of thinkers like Don Miguel Ruiz and his son's books. If I were to start over, I would read in this order, "The Four Agreements," "The Fifth Agreement," "The Five Levels of Attachment," "The Mastery of Self," "The Mastery of Love," "The Circle of Fire," "The Voice of Knowledge," and "The Three Questions."

The quest for self-understanding is not about casting aside our identity but about expanding our perception of it. It's about recognizing that we are more than the sum of our experiences and the roles we play. It's about waking up from the narratives we've authored about ourselves and embracing the full spectrum of our being. The journey may be challenging, but the rewards of self-awareness and inner peace are immeasurable. So, I pose this final question: What do you have to lose in seeking the true essence of your being?

Your Story

Identity Illusions: Are You Who You Think You Are?

Frank Ocean gifted us with this beautiful question, "What's a God to a non-believer, who don't believe in... Anything?" (Kanye West & Jay Z) This profound inquiry beckons us to ponder the essence of belief and identity. What does it mean to hold a belief or an identity in a world where everyone shares the same viewpoint? If every person on earth proclaimed themselves a Christian, would the term 'Christian' retain its significance? Similarly, what would it mean to be left if no one is to the right of you? You could try to identify yourself as a left wing person but you would be the farthest to the right.

This dilemma underscores a crucial aspect of self-identity: it is often defined in contrast to others. Our understanding of who we are gains richness and depth when mirrored against those who differ from us. Imagine a world where everyone shares your opinions, beliefs, and lifestyle. In such a scenario, the contours of your identity would blur, lacking the sharpness provided by the presence of differing views. The diversity of thought and belief, then, is not just a societal asset but a cornerstone in the architecture of individual identity.

When contemplating what it means to be human, our minds do not immediately jump to our basic functions – the fact that we have skin, breathe, and eat. Such characteristics, while essential, do not distinguish us in a meaningful way from other living creatures. Instead, we delve into attributes that set us apart from the animal kingdom: our ability to weave complex narratives, establish intricate governments, and nurture profound emotional connections. These elements speak to a deeper understanding of our humanity, an understanding that thrives on differentiation and uniqueness.

This brings us to a personal reflection on identity. If your sense of self – be it as a parent, a child, a lover, or an emotional being – is validated only in comparison to others, how authentic is it? How often have you encountered people who deny your self-perception, claiming it does not align with their preconceived notions of who you should be? If faced with a chorus of voices denying your claimed identity, do you concede to their view, or do you cling steadfastly to your self-concept?

Western culture often emphasizes the pursuit of a definitive, true self. But this quest is complicated by the fluidity and relativity of identity. This brings to mind a profound saying: "Seeing is not believing, believing is seeing." This quote suggests that belief shapes our perception of reality. We don't just observe and then believe; we believe first, thereby shaping our perception of what we see.

Consider life as a cinematic masterpiece, where you are simultaneously the audience and the screenwriter. If you passively wait for your story to unfold, you might inadvertently find yourself living a narrative scripted by others – perhaps influenced by a parent, a teacher, or a societal figure, rather than authored by your own aspirations and desires.

Therefore, I propose an alternative approach: Start by believing in the version of the universe you wish to see. Embrace the identity you aspire to, believe in your self-conceptions, and then proceed to live as if these beliefs have already materialized. In the grand, unpredictable theater of the universe, there are no absolute guarantees. But ask yourself, what do you stand to lose by embracing this philosophy? In a world where identities are often reflections of contrasting beliefs and societal molds, choosing to believe in your narrative and living it boldly might just be the most authentic expression of self you can offer.

Your Story

Embarking on a Journey Through Illusion: The Paradox of Manifestation

My journey into the realm of manifestation began with an exploration of a simple, yet profound concept: the power of thought to create reality. This idea, which I encountered in transformative books like "The Secret" and "Think and Grow Rich," suggested that the life I dreamt of—fitness, wealth, success—was merely a thought away. It was a seductive notion, one that promised that all my desires were within reach if only I adhered to certain mental practices.

This newfound ideology didn't just change my perspective; it revolutionized my entire digital experience. YouTube's algorithms, sensing my shift in interests, flooded my feed with stories of individuals who, through the power of manifesting, had sculpted their dream lives. I immersed myself in the teachings of people like Nevil Goddard and Joe Dispenza, dissecting hours of content in search of the formula that would unlock my desired reality.

The first major test of my commitment to this belief came in the form of a webinar. The host, an author whose work I had recently delved into, offered a roadmap to financial freedom for a staggering $25,000, discounted to $16,000 for immediate decision-makers. Although the offer was tempting, I initially declined. However, the very next day, I received a call with a new proposition: the same path to freedom for $20,000, a 20% discount, but this was my last chance.

❖

The salesperson's piercing questions about my fiancée's belief in me led me to a spontaneous decision: I increased my credit limit and purchased the program.

Fast forward two years, and the landscape of my life had drastically changed. I was now $60,000 in debt, having poured my resources into additional coaching, programs, and seminars. Yet, despite my unwavering commitment and financial sacrifices, my mentors had vanished, leaving me stranded in a sea of unanswered calls and broken promises. In a moment of despair, I found myself gazing at the sky, pondering the path that had led me here. I had believed fervently, invested every dime I had, yet here I was, burdened with maxed-out credit cards and devoid of guidance.

During this period of suffering, my reading material shifted subtly but significantly. Titles like "The Four Agreements," "Man's Search For Meaning," "As A Man Thinketh," "The Courage To Be Disliked," and "The Power of Now" offered me new perspectives. They prompted a critical, unasked question: If the world is an illusion, why was I so desperate to acquire wealth and social acceptance? Was I still mistakenly seeking peace outside myself? Had my trust in these mentors inadvertently led me to equate the acquisition of wealth with the attainment of freedom?

The answer was simpler and more profound than I had ever imagined. My lifelong quest had been a search for peace, yet I had led myself into believing that peace was a commodity, attainable through the materialization of personal desires. This journey, albeit painful, served as a humbling reminder that peace was always within me, not in the external achievements I had been chasing.

This epiphany led to a revolutionary understanding of manifestation. Perhaps its true essence was not about materializing things but about fostering states of being—peace, joy, happiness, gratitude, and thankfulness. What if these were the true treasures that could be manifested at any moment? What if visualizing a state of peace was the prerequisite to experiencing it?

This contemplation brings forth a crucial realization: by focusing our minds on peace and internal contentment, perhaps the external world aligns itself in mysterious, harmonious ways. As I reflected on individuals in dire circumstances, yearning for basic needs like freedom or clean water, I wondered: did they not manifest their desires due to a lack of intense wanting or visualization?

The journey through the labyrinth of manifestation thus reveals a more profound truth. Perhaps manifestation is less about attracting specific outcomes and more about cultivating a mindset that embraces peace, joy, and gratitude. By shifting our focus to these internal states, we might find that life unfolds exactly as it is meant to—gracefully and effortlessly. In this realization, I discovered that the true power of manifestation lies not in bending the external world to our will but in transforming our internal world, a world where peace and contentment reign supreme.

Your Story

How To Never Have Your Time Wasted Again

How often have we found ourselves frustrated over perceived wasted time? Be it in a job, a relationship, or other life experiences, the statement "I can't believe I wasted my time" is a familiar one, especially when our dreams and expectations don't align with reality. This sentiment, however, can be the catalyst for a profound awakening, a shift in perspective that could radically alter our outlook on life. Let me illustrate this with a personal anecdote.

I recall the painful end of my engagement, a time when I was engulfed in heartbreak. Walking away from what I thought was my future, I felt like I had wasted precious years. All the dreams and plans I had seemed to dissipate into thin air. At that moment, I had believed that the outcome I hoped for, the 'end', justified all the means, including the time invested. This belief, I later realized, was a limiting one.

This mindset is not uncommon. Many of us fixate on desired outcomes, enduring the present moment as merely a means to an end. We sacrifice today in the hope that tomorrow will bring the fulfillment of our dreams. But what happens when these dreams don't materialize? Why do we, as a culture, often defer our peace and happiness to a future that may never come?

❖

For years, I viewed romantic relationships as sacrifices made for a future dream. This perspective left me in a state of chronic dissatisfaction, punctuated by fleeting moments of joy. It was only when I began to see past relationships not as failed ventures but as gifts that I could embrace a more positive and fulfilling life.

Consider the common scenario of people working tirelessly, longing for the weekend, holidays, or vacations. Think about relationships where partners are on autopilot, rehashing the same arguments, plagued by the same insecurities, all in the hope of a proposal or a significant change from the other person. This way of living isn't inherently wrong, but it begs the question: If we desire something different, why not adopt a new perspective?

Who taught us that life is about sacrificing the present for a dream future? And what happens when that future doesn't turn out as we hoped? The prevalent mindset views life as a series of sacrifices, but what if we could shift this paradigm? What if we engaged in work and relationships not as chores or burdens but as expressions of self-love and paths to fulfillment?

The saying, "When life gives you lemons, make lemonade" suggests making the best out of an unwanted situation. But I propose a different view: Life gives you precisely what you plant. So why plant lemons if you don't desire lemonade? Instead, why not cultivate a life where every moment is cherished, where work and relationships are not seen as sacrifices but as opportunities to experience joy and fulfillment? What if we could say, "Life gives you exactly what you plant." The question is, why would you plant lemons and not be grateful that life gave you the ingredients to make chick filet's best beverage?

This message may not resonate with everyone. It's not intended for the masses, but it could be exactly what you need to hear. Imagine living a life where every moment is embraced, where the journey is as valued as the destination. This is not just about making the best of what you have; it's about creating a life you don't need to escape from.

So, why not wake up and live the life of your dreams in the here and now? The question isn't just about dreaming of a better future but about finding beauty and purpose in the present. It's a call to action, an invitation to shift your perspective and plant the seeds for a life that fulfills you every day. Wake up to your dreams.

Your Story

Unconditional Love Isn't About Them

Unconditional love often emerges as a complex and widely misunderstood concept. Many people labor under the misconception that loving oneself or others unconditionally implies bestowing affection that hasn't been rightfully earned. This notion suggests a kind of charity of the heart, extended in spite of a lack of deservingness. However, such an understanding grossly misrepresents the true essence and transformative power of unconditional love.

Unconditional love is less about the recipient and more about the giver's journey towards self-realization and inner harmony. It's about recognizing and embracing your own worth, as well as the worth of others, without conditions or limitations. This form of love is not a trophy awarded for achievements or good behavior; it's a fundamental acknowledgment of inherent value.

Consider the daily routines and challenges that often feel like burdens - working out, enduring a less-than-ideal job, or striving to maintain challenging relationships. These can be perceived as tiresome chores, necessitating sacrifice and self-coercion to mold into a 'better' version of oneself. Such a perspective stems from a feeling of inadequacy, as if one's current state isn't enough. However, when these tasks are approached from a place of self-love, the narrative changes dramatically. Choosing to engage in these activities because you love and value yourself transforms them into expressions of self-care and gratitude. This perspective shift turns obligations into opportunities, reflecting a deep appreciation for the mere chance to experience and grow.

Extending this unconditional love to others further enhances its transformative impact. It involves accepting people as they are, without the need for comprehension or justification. This isn't about doing someone else a favor; it's about creating a space for personal growth and openness to life's myriad possibilities. When you love unconditionally, you lay the foundation for fearlessly embracing change, especially when presented with perspectives or opportunities that resonate deeply. This approach to relationships can subtly steer you towards the life you've always dreamt of, often without conscious realization.

Unconditional love also catalyzes a profound shift in understanding and fulfilling personal needs. The relentless pursuit of external validation and acceptance, often marketed as the key to happiness and fulfillment, loses its allure. Realizing that all you ever needed resides within you, the need for external acquisitions diminishes. This doesn't mean withdrawing from societal norms or consumerism; instead, it means engaging with the world from a place of joy and love, not from a void seeking transient satisfaction.

This paradigm shift reveals a fundamental truth: life, in its essence, has always been perfect. The quest for external validation and acceptance is a mirage, obscuring the peace and happiness that naturally emanate from unconditional love. Embracing this form of love is akin to unlocking a path to freedom. It allows you to give generously from a place of abundance, supports your journey towards inner peace, and empowers you to live authentically.

The crux of unconditional love lies in its ability to transform not only personal experiences but also how we interact with the world. It's an invitation to stop chasing an elusive future and start embracing the present in its fullness. Are you ready to embark on this journey of self-discovery and fulfillment? The transition from dreaming about an ideal life to actively living it is a bold step, one that unconditional love makes not only possible but deeply rewarding.

Your Story

Life or Lifestyle:The Pursuit of Our Dream Existence

When we delve into the aspirations of people from various walks of life, we uncover a tapestry of dreams and desires. There are those who yearn for a simpler existence, longing to disconnect and immerse themselves in the tranquility of wilderness. Others envision a life of perpetual motion, traversing the globe and soaking in its beautiful cultures. Many look forward to the golden years of retirement, while some seek the profound connection of sharing their journey with a significant other. This spectrum of dreams encapsulates the diverse human experience, with each individual navigating their path towards these aspirations. However, a common thread weaves through these dreams – the notion of waiting, saving, and hoping for a future where these desires materialize. But, what if the possibility of living your dream exists in the here and now, without the need for deferment?

Consider the numerous occasions when you've expressed or even silently thought, "I would give anything to have that life." If such a desire is genuine, why then do we hesitate to commit fully to achieving it? My own journey mirrors this sentiment. I often found myself voicing these desires, oblivious to the fact that what held me back was not my circumstances, but my own beliefs about what was necessary for that life. Our understanding of lifestyle is multifaceted and deeply personal. For some, it's a quest to disprove doubters from our past, meticulously crafting a life that serves as a testament to our triumphs. For others, it's about tailoring retirement and vacations to fit a specific mold, complete with predefined destinations, comforts, and experiences. Even in the realm of relationships, we often find ourselves shackled by criteria that bear little relevance to the essence of building a meaningful partnership.

An interesting perspective emerges when considering those who prioritize creating a secure and specific lifestyle for their children. If one's own life is devoid of joy and fulfillment, is that the legacy we wish to bequeath to our offspring? Wouldn't it be more valuable to exemplify the pursuit of dreams and the realization of one's deepest desires? Reflect on the number of potential soulmates who might have crossed your path, only to be overlooked because they didn't fit a preconceived notion of an ideal partner. This dilemma highlights a paradox prevalent in Western culture – the perpetual quest for external validation, peace, and happiness, which often leads to a feeling of trading significant parts of ourselves, especially time, in pursuit of a future lifestyle that aligns with our dreams.

Maybe the key to unlocking the life of your dreams lies within the present moment. The barriers are not external circumstances but internal – our beliefs, expectations, and attachments to what we deem necessary for that dream life. We enter this world free, only to be laden with societal and cultural chains that dictate our course. These chains, though intangible, are potent, tethering us to a path well-trodden by others but not necessarily suited to our unique journey. The quintessential question then arises: Are you prepared to relinquish the idea of an idealized lifestyle in order to embrace and live the life you truly desire, starting now?

In essence, the dichotomy between life and lifestyle is not merely about choosing one over the other. It's about understanding that the pursuit of a lifestyle should not overshadow the essence of living. It's about recognizing that the true fulfillment of our dreams is not in the distant future but can be a tangible reality in our present. It's about breaking free from the chains of conventional expectations and daring to live a life that resonates with our deepest aspirations and values. As we navigate this journey, the realization dawns that the greatest gift we can offer ourselves and those we love is not a meticulously crafted lifestyle, but the freedom and courage to live authentically, passionately, and unapologetically in pursuit of our dreams.

Your Story

Understanding the Difference Between Companionship and Relationships

In many Western societies, the notion of unconditional self-love is not deeply ingrained. Instead, love and acceptance are often conditional, tied to fulfilling certain obligations or conforming to societal norms. This conditional approach to self-love extends its influence to our relationships with others. If our love for ourselves is contingent upon meeting certain standards, we are likely to impose similar conditions on our love and acceptance of others. In this context, authentic relationships—those that truly reflect who we are—become challenging to maintain. In my personal journey, I found myself recoiling from the true reflection of myself that emerged in my relationships, whether they were romantic or platonic. This aversion led me to opt for companionship, a less demanding and more superficial form of interaction, over deeper, more meaningful relationships.

Dr. Shante Holley, a noted expert in the field, provides a clear delineation between companionship and relationships. According to Dr. Holley, A companionship is a plus one, a good time, a few laughs, somebody to fill the time, "let's spend some time together, let's meet up and have some drinks"… it's very low stakes and there is no emotional commitment. Companionship is embedded in a relationship, but a relationship is not necessarily embedded in companionship. A relationship requires someone to be emotionally available. It requires fidelity, vulnerability, accountability, honesty, integrity, truthful communication, and an investment of self. A relationship is very high stakes and this is an emotional investment being made.

Confronted with the need to accept myself and others as we truly are, I found myself gravitating towards companionship to fill the voids in my life. This choice allowed me to avoid dealing with the deeper issues of trauma, pain, and struggle that I was not ready to face. Something western culture does not realize is that most of our perceived relationships are companionships.. It's common to feel misunderstood or even betrayed when friends or significant others highlight our flaws, leading to conflicts and estrangements. Personally, I found it easier to connect with children and animals, as they didn't challenge my defenses or force me to confront my issues.

The questions I'm posing to you today are challenging, and it might be uncomfortable, but they are questions I had to confront in my own life to let go and find peace. Questions like, Could I be the problem? Is the reason I have not found lasting love because of me? Am I not ready to love someone completely because even though I say I love myself, there are sides of me I am not ready to come to terms with? Am I projecting gaslighting on my friends? I believe you should always protect yourself from others hurting you, but maybe your relationships haven't worked because you are only ready for companionship. Only you hold the keys to the answer. Protecting oneself from hurt is natural, but it's possible that my relationships have faltered because I was only ready for companionship, not a committed relationship.

I invite you to introspect and question the nature of your relationships. Are they mere companionships, or do they represent something deeper? The journey towards understanding these dynamics is not just about others; it's fundamentally about you. It's about confronting your fears, acknowledging your flaws, and embracing the possibility of transformation. By unlocking the door to self-awareness and emotional maturity, you pave the way for more authentic and fulfilling relationships. The key to this transformation lies within you. Are you ready to awaken from the nightmare of unfulfilled connections to live the life of your dreams?

Your Story

Exploring the True Essence
of the Golden Rule

The "Golden Rule" emerges as a universally acknowledged belief: treat others as you would wish to be treated. At its core, this principle beckons us to a journey of empathy and mutual respect. Yet, its application often skims the surface, overshadowed by a lack of introspection and a misunderstanding of its profound depth.

Traditionally, the Golden Rule is seen as a straightforward directive: act towards others in a way that mirrors your own desires and expectations. However, this interpretation is mired in subjectivity. People's actions are frequently guided by what they assume others need, based on their own desires and beliefs. For example, individuals with strong religious convictions might view the Golden Rule as a call to evangelize, believing that sharing their spiritual truth is the greatest service they can offer, as it mirrors their own desires.

This approach, however, raises an essential question: does this form of projection truly honor the spirit of the Golden Rule? Is it genuinely empathetic to impose one's beliefs or truths onto another, under the guise of doing unto others? Such actions often stem from a disregard for the individuality and autonomy of others, assuming that one's truth is universally applicable. In doing so, we risk alienating others, pushing our perspectives while neglecting to consider what they genuinely need or want.

The essence of the Golden Rule might be better realized through a more nuanced approach. Imagine a world where the primary desire is not to project our truths but to foster genuine connections. This involves taking a sincere interest in others, seeking to understand and accept them for who they are. It means being transparent and vulnerable, sharing our own lives and intentions openly. Such a stance fosters a culture of respect and trust, transcending the boundaries of differing beliefs.

In Western cultures, there's often a sense of resignation—a belief that adjusting one's behavior for the greater good is futile because others won't reciprocate. This cynicism leads to a transactional view of human interactions, where actions are valued only if they yield specific, desired outcomes. Such a perspective breeds a conditional form of empathy, contingent on the return it generates.

This brings us to a pivotal introspection: Do we act with vulnerability and transparency merely in hopes of reciprocation, or because these qualities authentically resonate with our principles? What if we could pivot our intentions inward, focusing on understanding, accepting, and loving ourselves? By nurturing self-love, we can extend genuine affection and empathy to others, not out of a need for reciprocation, but because we inherently possess love to give. In this light, reciprocity becomes a natural byproduct, not a prerequisite.

Imagine if we reframed the Golden Rule from a place of self-fulfillment. If we were content and self-sufficient, what would we then desire from others? Perhaps the answer lies not in specific actions or words, but in a broader ethos of empathy and understanding. When we act from a place of inner fulfillment, our interactions with others are not transactions but expressions of our innate humanity.

The true power of the Golden Rule lies not in its literal application, but in its potential to guide us towards deeper self-awareness and universal empathy. It challenges us to look beyond our immediate desires and to consider the unique needs and perspectives of others. In doing so, it becomes more than a rule—it transforms into a beacon of compassion and understanding, guiding us towards a more empathetic and connected world.

Your Story

Life Uncomplicated
Rediscovering Joy in the Basics

In our quest to understand existence, we often stumble upon a profound realization: the universe, in its vast expanse, operates on principles of fundamental simplicity. This notion challenges our deeply ingrained belief that life is inherently complex. It prompts us to ponder whether this complexity is a product of the universe itself or a consequence of our attempts to articulate its nature.

Our minds, analytical and detail-oriented, act as tools of dissection, slicing the world into segments we can understand. We label, categorize, and define, driven by a desire to bring order to the chaos of existence. But in doing so, do we inadvertently complicate what is inherently simple? Are we, in our quest for comprehension and control, distorting the true essence of life?

This introspection leads to a crucial question: Could our happiness be rooted in our ability to accept life as it is, in its most basic and unembellished form? Often, we divide our experiences into 'good' or 'bad,' crafting narratives around these labels. But if we pause to question this habitual segmentation, might we find that the problems we perceive are not as dire as they seem?

The present moment, when examined, often reveals a lack of inherent negativity. This realization ushers in a state of acceptance, where life is not a series of issues to be resolved but a current to be experienced. In this flow, we find the simplicity that might be key to our contentment and peace.

This philosophy is not about passive resignation to life's circumstances. Instead, it represents an active engagement with the present, a deliberate choice to experience life without superimposing our judgments and narratives upon it. This approach does not deny the existence of challenges or suffering. Rather, it proposes a shift in how we interact with these facets of life. By embracing the simplicity of existence, we might discover that what we need most is not a radical change or an escape but a new perspective on what already is.

The idea of simplicity in a complex world is both a reminder and an invitation. It prompts us to consider whether our unhappiness stems from life's nature or our responses to it. It encourages us to reflect on whether our efforts to dissect and categorize life's experiences might be distancing us from the inherent joy and simplicity of being.

As we navigate our daily lives, filled with their various intricacies, we might do well to remember this fundamental truth: life, at its core, is simple. It is our perceptions, our incessant need to categorize and control, that introduce complexity. Acknowledging this can open us to a reality where each moment is not a challenge to overcome but an experience to be embraced.

In essence, this perspective on life is a call to embrace its simplicity. It challenges us to reevaluate our tendencies to overanalyze and overcomplicate, urging us to find contentment in the present moment. These insights are not just philosophical musings; they are practical tools for a more fulfilling existence. By accepting life's simplicity, we might just find that what we have been seeking has always been right in front of us, in its most pure and unadorned form.

Perhaps if we could wake up from the dream of complexity, we could wake up to the simplicity of life.

Your Story

Embracing Pain: A Paradigm Shift in Western Culture's Quest for Comfort

In the intricate fabric of Western culture there exists a quest: the quest to eradicate pain. This pursuit, deeply embedded in our societal norms, prompts a reflection on our perception of pain. We develop medicines to dull physical agony and mental distress, effectively blocking the signals that inform our brain of our struggles. Yet, this relentless battle against pain begs a critical question: Are we viewing pain through a misguided lens?

Consider for a moment the undeniable truth that change is often born out of discomfort. The very essence of transformation is intertwined with the experience of pain. Reflect on your life—how many times have you stood on the precipice of change, ready to embrace a new habit or lifestyle, only to retreat into the comfort of the familiar? This phenomenon raises a legitimate inquiry: Are we, in our aversion to pain, inadvertently stalling our potential for growth?

Imagine a world devoid of pain and loss. At first glance, this utopia brims with potential for unparalleled achievement and happiness. But delve deeper, and ask yourself: In the absence of pain, what would drive us to grow, to change? In moments of sheer joy—whether at a concert, with loved ones, or in the throes of passion—are we inclined to contemplate significant life changes? And if fortune were to bestow upon us untold wealth, would our aspirations extend beyond the mere spending of our riches?

Could it be that life, in its infinite wisdom, has structured itself precisely as it should? Pain and loss, far from being mere hindrances, might be essential components of our journey. They serve as reminders of what could be, urging us to persevere, to explore uncharted paths of personal development.

Pain plays a critical role in shaping our decisions and life paths. Often, it is the discomfort of our current circumstances that propels us towards change. The decision to pursue a healthier lifestyle, to foster more fulfilling relationships, or to embark on a journey of self-improvement is frequently triggered by a sense of dissatisfaction or discomfort.

Embracing pain does not imply seeking it out or wallowing in suffering. It means acknowledging pain, understanding its role, and learning from it. By shifting our perspective from avoidance to acceptance, we open ourselves to a deeper understanding of our experiences and a more resilient approach to life's challenges.

There is a symbiotic relationship between pain and personal development. Pain can act as a catalyst, pushing us out of our comfort zones and into realms of greater self-awareness and fulfillment. It challenges us to confront our fears, to overcome our limitations, and to grow in ways we might never have imagined.

As you reflect on this discourse, consider your own journey with pain. How has it shaped your life? What lessons have you gleaned from your encounters with discomfort? This is not just a theoretical exploration but a call to action—a prompt to reassess your relationship with pain and, in doing so, to potentially unlock new avenues of personal growth and fulfillment.

In reevaluating our relationship with pain, we may discover that it is not an enemy to be vanquished, but a complex, multifaceted phenomenon with the potential to transform us. It is an integral part of the human experience, one that can teach us, shape us, and propel us towards a richer, more nuanced understanding of life. The question, then, is not how we can eliminate pain, but how we can learn from it and grow with it.

Your Story

Illuminating the Darkness:
A Journey from Despair to Hope

In the profound journey of life, we often find ourselves in moments of darkness, akin to being in a dimly lit room. It's in these moments, where it seems the light has been extinguished, that we're gifted with an incredible opportunity. As the eyes of our soul adjust to this darkness, we begin to perceive a light that had always been there, yet remained unnoticed.

Imagine life as a room bathed in light, with rays of sunshine streaming through the windows. When the room is bright, the gentle light from the windows merges seamlessly into the background. In such an environment, the necessity to explore beyond the room diminishes. Even in a room where darkness begins to creep in, the minimal light present is often just enough to give us a glimpse of our surroundings. We grow so accustomed to this room, our comfort zone, that even when we could embrace the light, we often don't. Our focus remains fixated on what's familiar, what's known.

My own journey through the darkest phases of my life began in the most unexpected of places – lying on the floor of my kitchen. It was there that I realized the need for a monumental shift in my life. The darkness I was in was not just a lack of light; it was a profound, painful void. Interestingly, it wasn't the absolute darkest point, but it was the start of a journey of transformation, one that I am still navigating.

Embarking on a journey of change isn't about seeking perfection or experiencing a single, life-altering moment that instantly transforms everything. It's a series of steps, sometimes stumbles, in the darkness. I recall vividly the feeling of moving around in that room, bumping into things, each collision a metaphor for the challenges faced. Lying there, immersed in my pain and tears, I didn't have to do anything. I could simply be in my pain, my suffering, my sorrow.

But the process of standing up, of finding a way out of that room, was fraught with difficulty. Each step was a struggle, filled with uncertainty and pain. Stepping out of that room and into a new space, a space where nothing was familiar, was challenging. I found myself lost, disconnected from who I had been. It was in this chaos, this unknown territory, that the seeds of change began to take root.

To those who are experiencing their own periods of darkness, I want to extend a message of hope. There is always light, even if it seems faint or distant. It's not just about seeing the light but being willing to look for it. This light is a symbol of hope, a constant presence in our lives. I am here with you on this journey, a companion in understanding and shared experience. Remember, you are never alone in your quest. My heart and my support are with you. If you ever feel the need to reach out, to share your story, or seek comfort, my social media pages and email are always open. You are loved, and together, we can navigate our way towards the light, finding strength and transformation in the journey itself.

Let this journey be a testament to the power of change, to the resilience of the human spirit. Embrace the light, embrace the change, and remember, in the deepest darkness, the light shines the brightest.

Your Story

Love Beyond Consumerism

In a world increasingly dominated by consumerism, where the pursuit of what we don't have takes center stage, it's no wonder that our approach to love has been influenced by this desire for acquisition. The concept of love in modern culture often raises an interesting questions: What does it mean to find love, and what does it mean to be loved? Many people confess to understanding how to give love, yet struggle with loving themselves. This paradox raises an essential inquiry: How can one recognize the love they seek without having experienced it personally?

Our societal narrative frequently emphasizes the desire to be loved. People yearn for a best friend, a partner to navigate life's challenges, someone who provides what they lack independently. This longing often manifests in the search for a 'better half', a notion that inadvertently implies incompleteness without this significant other. But what criteria define this elusive other half? How do we know when we've found them, and what will they contribute to our lives that signifies their vital role?

In a culture obsessed with self-validation, love has arguably transformed into the ultimate measure of worth. The status of being engaged, married, or associated with a group often overshadows the genuine pursuit of compatible companionship. This societal pressure can lead to compromising decisions in relationships, such as giving ultimatums, remaining in unfulfilling partnerships, or hastening into parenthood with partners you eventually drift apart from. This tendency might stem from viewing others as a means to fulfill a personal narrative of self-identity. Can one truly love another for who they are if they are more enamored with the idea of who they could become with that person? And does the identity of the partner matter as much as their willingness to fit into the narrative we believe we deserve?

Reflecting on personal experiences, I once believed that I loved others despite a lack of self-love. However, I now recognize that what I offered was not genuine love but rather an expression of my desire to be loved in return. This approach prevented me from seeing people for who they truly were, focusing instead on what they could offer me. This realization dawned upon me when I recognized that my love was conditional, dependent on how well others met my expectations or loved me in the way I desired. Once these conditions were not met, my affection waned.

The journey towards unconditional self-love marked a turning point. It revealed the conditional nature of my acceptance of others and helped me recognize the love others were offering, which I had previously been unable to accept due to my inner shortcomings. While material needs are straightforward, with clear solutions, intangible needs like love are more complex. Many of us are influenced by cinematic portrayals of love, expecting to recognize it instantly when it arrives. While some may be fortunate enough to experience such a serendipitous encounter, for others, love may not be a matter of chance but rather a journey of self-discovery and intentional understanding.

Perhaps for those not blessed with serendipitous love, the path involves learning to love oneself unconditionally, understanding personal needs, and loving others in the way we wish to be loved, devoid of expectations. This self-love might be the key to unlocking the love we seek, transforming our approach from a search for what we lack to an appreciation and acceptance of what we already possess.

I love the shows: Love Is Blind, The Ultimatum, and 90 day fiancé as much as the next, but the quest for love in a consumer-driven culture is fraught with misconceptions and unrealistic expectations. The journey to finding true love might very well begin with a journey within, understanding and loving oneself unconditionally. Only then can we hope to find and recognize the love we seek, not as a commodity to complete us, but as a complementary addition to the wholeness we already embody.

Your Story

Whose Story Are You Living?

In life, we are often handed scripts, narratives that sculpt our ego and convince us of the roles we must play. These scripts, intricate and persuasive, dictate not just actions but beliefs about who we are meant to be. Reflecting on my own life's journey, I think a lot about the essence of these roles – what does it truly mean to be 'black', a 'good guy', an 'athlete', or 'healing'? I question, are these identities mere self-fulfilling prophecies, born from a belief that life must unfold in certain predetermined ways?

Healing, for instance, is often portrayed as a journey rife with pain. The pursuit of health is painted as a relentless struggle, while relationships are framed as inherently complicated. This pervasive narrative, handed down by parents, teachers, and culture, seems to suggest that life must be a certain way – a testament that the struggle is, indeed, worth it. But here lies the critical inquiry: when does the journey of healing end if one's identity is eternally tethered to the state of 'healing', finding solace and connection only in shared suffering?

It dawns upon us that perhaps, we were indoctrinated to believe certain truths about life and our experiences before we even had the chance to choose. But with this awakening, a new idea emerges. Now aware of the possibility that these beliefs might have been mere constructs, we stand at a crossroads. what kind of life do you want to gift the rest of your time?

I'm sure you've heard it, "transforming our life's narrative is not an overnight endeavor. It requires a deliberate and conscious departure from long-standing patterns." Yet, within this introspection lies a fundamental question: if we truly know what we desire most, why not embody that version of ourselves every day? Why not embrace unconditional self-love, empowering us to choose, day after day, the identity that resonates most authentically with our being?

This call to action is not merely a change in behavior but a revolution of the soul. It is about breaking free from the chains of preconceived notions and societal constructs. It is an invitation to dance to the rhythm of our own drum, to paint our canvas with colors of our choosing, to write our own story – not as actors playing a part, but as playwrights of our destiny.

In this grand narrative of life, we are reminded that the most powerful stories are those we write for ourselves. They are the stories that emerge not from a script given to us, but from the depths of our own consciousness and the courage to live authentically. As we embark on this journey of self-discovery and transformation, we are not just redefining our identity but reimagining the very essence of what it means to live.

Your Story

Why Does Free Will Matter?

Few threads are as intricately woven and as endlessly fascinating as the question of free will. It's a topic that has perplexed scholars, theologians, and thinkers across ages and cultures, serving as a centerpiece for debates both profound and perennial.

The Christian perspective offers a unique duality: the belief in a Creator who knew us before our inception, yet endowed us with the gift of choice. This theological standpoint posits a divine plan, a predestined path laid out by an omniscient God. Yet, paradoxically, it also champions the human ability to steer our own course. This raises a pivotal question: if our paths are preordained by a celestial architect, do our choices carry any real weight? In contrast, an agnostic viewpoint strips away the divine overseer and places humanity at the helm of its destiny. This school of thought suggests that our lives are not guided by a divine hand, but rather, are the sum of our choices, random events, and the chaos of existence.

I don't think what you believe about free will matters as much as why you believe it. How does believing in or not believing in free will sculpt our decision-making process? If one subscribes to the notion of free choice, does this empower them to make different, perhaps braver, decisions? Conversely, if one believes in a divinely orchestrated path, does this instill a sense of resignation, or perhaps comfort, in their choices?

Perhaps we are astray in our questioning. The real inquiry, then, is not about the existence of free will, but about our reaction to the choices we face. Daily, we are besieged by decisions - some demanding immediate reaction, others allowing the luxury of contemplation. In these moments, do we feel constricted, limited to a handful of options, or do we feel the exhilarating freedom of endless possibilities?

Why then, should we not revel in these decisions, regardless of the underpinning philosophy of free will? Why succumb to disappointment, frustration, or anger? It's plausible that our belief, or disbelief, in free will serves as a convenient scapegoat for the decisions we make, absolving us from the weight of responsibility or the pangs of regret.

Ultimately, the question circles back to you. What drives you to make the decisions you do? Is it a quest for meaning, a reaction to external stimuli, or perhaps an unconscious adherence to a prewritten script you are unaware of? This quest for understanding our decision-making process, in the grand scheme of free will, is perhaps the most enlightening journey of all.

The question of free will is not just a philosophical quandary but a mirror reflecting our deepest fears, hopes, and the very essence of what it means to be human. It challenges us to introspect, to question, and perhaps, in the end, to simply embrace the beautiful complexity of our existence.

Your Story

How To Have Everything You Want

We find ourselves constantly in pursuit of something more – a loving partner, adorable children, the allure of wealth, the comfort of a home. Yet, in this relentless chase, we often forget to pause and think: Why do these desires resonate so deeply within us? Is it a mere reflection of our lifelong dreams, or is there a more profound reason that these aspirations hold such sway over our hearts and minds?

We entered this world cradled in peace, yet as time's wheel turned, we were indoctrinated with a curious notion: to attain peace, one must fulfill their external wants and needs. This philosophy finds its roots in Maslow's Hierarchy of Needs, a brainchild born from our collective yearning.

The Western world, in its feverish dream, has long cultivated an insatiable hunger for more. It's a siren call, luring us to borrow from the present, to empower ourselves to chase the future we envision in our most vivid dreams. We are led to believe that the key to rediscovering our lost peace lies in externalities – the love we yearn for, the familial bonds we crave, the wealth to dissolve our troubles.

Yet, this begs the question: Why do we seek external solutions for internal tranquility?

As children, simplicity reigned. Our needs were fundamental – nourishment, care, rest. In those tender years, even the absence of some needs didn't diminish our capacity for joy. Who among us hasn't seen a child, diaper full, yet utterly absorbed in play or slumber? When did the pursuit of money, relationships, and a myriad of other desires start eclipsing our life's joy? When did our inability to immediately fulfill our deepest desires begin casting such a long shadow over our happiness?

I recall days spent in coffee shops or restless in bed, haunted by the ghosts of unfulfilled wishes and paths not taken. In those moments, no action could bridge the gap between desire and reality, yet this chasm robbed me of my peace. My existence was a battleground, marred by depression, stress, and suffering.

The revelation came not in acquiring what I lacked but in understanding the significance I attached to these voids. It dawned on me that the absence of my desires didn't disrupt my peace; rather, it was the meaning I ascribed to this absence that was the true thief of serenity.

We all possess the innate ability to discover peace in the present. Viktor Frankl, along with other authors who have traversed through living hells, stand as testaments to this truth. The transformative query that altered my perspective was, "What am I gaining by not choosing peace in this moment?" The moment one unravels the truth behind this question, an awakening ensues.

Life's journey isn't about amassing external treasures. True fulfillment and peace are found within, in understanding and redefining our relationship with our desires and the meanings we attach to them. It's a journey inward, to the core of our being, where the serene waters of contentment and fulfillment reside, waiting to be discovered.

What if instead of saying, "Once everything falls into place, I'll find peace" we said, "Once I find my peace, everything will fall into place."

Your Story

Thought 45

You Are Not Your Thoughts

As early as I can remember there's been this incessant, unyielding dialogue in my head. A voice, or voices, endlessly debating, reflecting, ruminating. This inner dialogue has been my constant companion. It dissects every glance, every interaction, and spins countless tales about past blunders and future dreams.

The communication in my head was often the loudest while taking a shower or laying in bed as I thought about all the things I wish I had done or should have done to create the future of my dreams. I thought about past choices, love lost, mistakes made, and worries about the future. My anxiety would peak in these moments and despite the fact that I was just laying in bed or trying to read a book my stress and depression levels almost always peaked.

But why... and how was it possible that the voice in my head could simultaneously take all sides at once. I remember when I first read the Untethered Soul, a book that helped me recognize that I was not any of the voices in my head. Not the critic, not the cheerleader, not the sage or the fool. But with that in mind, who am I?

Here's a line from the book that struck me like a thunderbolt: "There is nothing more important to true growth than realizing that you are not the voice of the mind - you are the one who hears it. (Singer)" A profound realization that to find happiness, one must release the grip of the inner dramatist.

The hardest part about recognizing that the voice in my head was not me was not that the voice was just chattering away for no reason but that I in some ways had come to love the drama that constantly unfolded in my head. The moments of lust, anxiety, stress, joy, and excitement all fueled by the chatter. When I finally got to a point that the talking started to slow I noticed a new depression.I was left in a peculiar state of emptiness. A void where once there was a relentless narrative.

I was faced with the uncertainty of not knowing what to do with myself. What was I supposed to feel in these moments when the constant chatter in my head, which had always helped me experience a range of emotions, was no longer there? What was I supposed to do with the emptiness that remained? The truth revealed itself, highlighting one of my greatest fears - more intense than depression, more overwhelming than my anxiety or stress - the fear that I wouldn't know who I was without the drama my brain had created. I felt empty.

In these moments, I was reminded that I had the opportunity to be grateful, to appreciate the life I had been given. I realized that I had been so absorbed in categorizing the world into segments I considered good, bad, stressful, or exciting, that I had overlooked the specialness of the present moment. The future will unfold, and the past offers lessons, but I can be grateful for what I have right now, and that is perfect.

You are perfect, and regardless of whether you believe the voice in your head is truly you, this moment remains perfect. I hope you awaken to its beauty.

Your Story

What Does It Mean To Suffer?

Suffering, an elusive and deeply personal experience, often evades definition. While pain is subjective, as evidenced by the question from doctors about pain on a scale from one to ten, suffering shares this trait. No two individuals experience suffering identically, even under seemingly identical circumstances. It's not uncommon for people to endure suffering in silence, presenting a facade of contentment until it becomes unbearable.

This phenomenon leads me to a perspective some may find controversial: Pain and suffering are inherently subjective because, at their core, they are a choice. My belief might seem counterintuitive. Often, it doesn't feel like a choice, and perhaps the decision on how we experience pain and suffering was made long before we understood its implications.

However, any phenomenon that is entirely subjective must be considered a choice. I stand by this assertion, as my life, as you will soon discover, has been a testament to this philosophy. For a long time, I suffered in silence. Outwardly, I was the quintessential happy person, always smiling in the company of others. Yet, internally, I was in turmoil, yearning for a different life, burdened by self-disappointment and a lack of self-understanding. My breakthrough came after delving into literature about the ego. I realized that my suffering had become an integral part of my identity. It was the conduit through which I connected with friends and embodied the stereotype of the 'good guy' who always finished last. In my mind, I was a victim.

This realization brought forth an unsettling question: Who would I be without my suffering? How would my relationships evolve if this aspect of my identity changed? Embracing the power of choice transformed everything. My friendships, love life, and most importantly, my relationship with myself, underwent profound changes. Letting go of my suffering was tantamount to shedding an old identity. The hardest part was acknowledging that my suffering was the last remnant of my past. It was a lens through which I viewed myself—a person defined by love and loss, failure and resilience. This suffering, while painful, was integral to my identity as Django. The thought of losing this connection to my past was, in some ways, more daunting than the suffering itself.

However, I recognize that everyone's journey is unique. For some, the role of suffering in life might never end. Yet, for those who resonate with my experience, I pose a fundamental question: What kind of life do you want to gift your time? If your life has been defined by suffering, know that this doesn't have to be a permanent state. Ultimately, the choice is yours. Whether to remain tethered to suffering or to embrace the potential for change is a decision that each of us must make, guided by our individual experiences and perspectives.

Your Story

Why Does What You Do Matter?

In Western culture, there is an overwhelming focus on what we do with our lives. But it's not just about our actions; it's also about how others perceive these actions. Historically, and even more so today, there's a fixation on the visible outcomes of our endeavors. This preoccupation has been magnified by social media, creating a scenario where many are more concerned with appearing a certain way to others, regardless of the reality behind the façade.

One must ponder why our culture places such importance on others' perceptions of our actions, often valuing these perceptions more than the actions themselves or, more importantly, the reasons behind them. The book "The Courage To Be Disliked" poses a thought-provoking question: if you were to pick up trash daily, unnoticed and unthanked, would you continue? This inquiry probes the core of our motivations. Do we act because we believe in the righteousness of our actions, or are we seeking external validation and praise? Would we still choose integrity if we knew our actions would remain unseen?

This brings us to a deeper question about the essence of goodness. Can we truly consider ourselves good if our actions are performed solely under the watchful eyes of others? And if we are willing to stray from our principles when unnoticed, what does that reveal about our true character?

❖

Are we really good people if we are only doing good when others know that we are doing good? Are we really good people if we are willing to do wrong when people are not looking? Who are we really as a culture? I remember realizing that I was not as good of a guy as I thought I was. I was transactional in my goodness. If it served me to be good I was all about it but if people did not respond the way I wanted them to or did not pay attention to my good deeds I grew frustrated with the fact that I was doing the right thing but was not getting what I wanted out of it. I couldn't help but think it would be a better life to not carry the responsibility if people were not going to congratulate me for being such a good person.

There was nothing good about me. I was rotten to the core. I was not interested in doing good because I believed in good, I was interested in doing good because I thought others were going to congratulate me and I would get more of what I wanted for being good. There have been times I have asked people questions about their lives and the reason for asking the exact same question to different people in distinct situations was completely different. For some I wanted them to hurt the way that I had, for others I was genuinely interested in them and wanted to learn more. In both cases what I did was the same but why I did it was not and this brings me to the point of this thought.

Perhaps the reasons behind our actions hold more significance than the actions themselves. True awareness awakens us to a state where causing harm to others becomes unthinkable. We no longer seek revenge or inflict pain, as these impulses arise from a state of unconsciousness, where we project our distorted views onto others. In a state of heightened awareness, our motives are rooted in unconditional love. We create limitations when we lose sight of the grander perspective that life offers.

As you navigate your journey, ask yourself what kind of life will you gift your time. And when you find that answer make sure to ask the even more important question, why? The answers to these questions will illuminate a path toward a life not driven by external applause but by the fulfillment that comes from aligning actions with profound, authentic intentions. Remember, it's not just what you do that matters, but why you do it. This understanding is key to living a purposeful, meaningful life.

Your Story

Living in a Dream:
Finding Joy in the Present

Do you ever find yourself lost in thought, longing for a time that may have never existed? We all have fantasies of an ideal life - one filled with adventure, meaning, and fulfillment. Yet chasing these dreams can rob us of joy in the here and now.

I'm certainly guilty of this. I'd reminisce about my carefree college days, back when the world seemed full of possibility. Or I'd daydream about an ambitious career that was never quite realized. The truth is, much of what I longed for was more imagination than memory. Sure, there were happy moments, but even those were airbrushed by nostalgia. I oftentimes focused on what I wished things were more than how they really were.

By fixating on an unrealistic past or future, I denied myself the chance to appreciate the present. Each moment offers its own potential for contentment, if only we open our eyes to it. This realization has allowed me to find more gratitude in my ordinary days. Though life may not align with my fanciful visions, it remains full of small wonders.

The thief of joy is neither the past nor the future, but our attachment to these imagined realities. If we let go of what might have been or could be, and embrace what is, we can fall in love with this moment. For this moment is all we ever have. Each breath and heartbeat is an opportunity to connect with life. When pining for other places and times, gently return your attention to now. You may be surprised at the peace and happiness waiting for you in the here and now. The life you're seeking is today's life, not yesterday's or tomorrow's. It's time to start living your dreams in the moment.

Your Story

Finding The Love You Seek

We often discuss love as though it were a rare and finite resource. Our relentless pursuit of this elusive emotion leaves us perpetually yearning, grasping, and yet, somehow, always falling short. This is a consequence of a prevailing belief that love is a scarce commodity, a delicate treasure we must seek from others. This viewpoint, that love resides outside of ourselves, breeds an insidious fear - the fear of losing what we so desperately desire.

When we accept love as a limited entity, we inevitably live in perpetual dread, our hearts held hostage by the ever-present anxiety that we might, at any moment, forfeit this precious asset. It becomes something we can gain only from the benevolence of others, and we convince ourselves that they possess just enough to bestow upon one lucky recipient. With this singular perspective, it is no wonder that we find ourselves ensnared in a web of stress, frustration, and mistrust, even when we are in the embrace of those we claim to love. A fraction of our consciousness remains locked in a state of anxiety, perpetually afraid of losing what we have so diligently sought.

Could this be the reason why individuals within meaningful, monogamous relationships often grow to despise one another more fervently than any other group? Perhaps these relationships are, in truth, more akin to companionships masquerading as relationships. People may not have truly loved each other for their genuine selves but rather for the services they provided. Once the expectations were unmet or the individuals failed to evolve in the desired direction, the illusion of love crumbled. But can one honestly claim to have loved another if the heart can turn from love to hatred in a mere moment? It's a question that leaves me in doubt, for I, personally, cannot comprehend such a shift. My devotion to self-love prevents me from choosing the darkness of hatred.

Why, then, do our hearts harbor such potent reservoirs of hatred when it comes to matters of love and relationships? What drives us to mistreat those we claim to cherish when they do not conform to our expectations? Why is it that couples who once shared a bed, raised children together, and exchanged vows of eternal love can eventually harbor profound animosity towards one another? These questions lead us to ponder whether our culture has truly grasped the essence of self-love, and until we can unravel this enigma, we may remain perpetually ensnared in this complex web of emotions.

In the labyrinth of our hearts, love is not a finite resource to be hoarded or feared. Rather, it is an infinite wellspring, residing within us, awaiting our recognition. Love is not something external, a gift that can be granted or revoked by another. It is an intrinsic part of our very being, a force that flows through us, radiating outward into the world. This realization shifts the paradigm, transforming love.

When we embrace the understanding that love begins with self-love, we unlock the potential for genuine, unconditional love for others. Self-love is not a selfish act but a necessary one. It empowers us to love without reservation, without fear of losing something external, because we recognize that love is a boundless energy that we can continuously generate from within. In this state of self-love, we no longer seek to possess or control others; instead, we extend our love freely, without attachment to outcomes or expectations.

As we embark on this transformative journey towards self-love, the dark clouds of hatred that once loomed over our relationships begin to dissipate. We understand that others are not responsible for our happiness, and we release them from the burdensome role of fulfilling our desires. Instead, we appreciate them for who they truly are, cherishing their uniqueness and accepting their imperfections. Love, in its purest form, is no longer dependent on their actions or conformity to our desires.

So, why do we experience hatred in matters of love and relationships? It is because we have strayed from the path of self-love, mistakenly believing that love is something we can extract from others. We have allowed our desires and expectations to cloud the purity of our hearts, leading us down a treacherous path of attachment and dependency.

To break free from this cycle of love and hatred, we must embark on a journey of self-discovery and self-acceptance. We must learn to love ourselves unconditionally, recognizing our worthiness and inherent value. As we nurture the flame of self-love within, it will naturally radiate outward, illuminating our relationships with the gentle warmth of genuine love.

Love is not a limited asset to be sought outside of ourselves, but an infinite wellspring that resides within. It is a force that flows freely when we embrace self-love and release the shackles of attachment and expectation. By embarking on the path of self-love, we can transcend the cycle of love and hatred, forging relationships based on acceptance, compassion, and unconditional love. Only then can we truly understand the profound essence of love and experience its boundless beauty in all its glory.

Your Story

Outro

If there's anything I wish for you, it's that between the lines of this book, you've managed to wake up. It's a peculiar thing, this awakening; every time I catch myself disliking an aspect of my life, I wonder, "Whose dream am I living in? Who taught me to live this way?" Reality, I've come to understand, is only what we believe it to be.

Embarking on change was no small feat for me. The thoughts "Who am I without these beliefs?" echoed in my mind, challenging the very fabric of my being. These beliefs and ideas were the architects of my identity for as long as I can remember. Yet, in the face of genuine unhappiness, I realized I had every right to discard them. We aren't bound to live out someone else's dream indefinitely; we have the power to wake up, to craft our own world. This world, albeit influenced by the language and cultural models we inherit, can become more ours through awareness and choice.

Through the process of writing this book and, I hope, through your reading of it, there's been an awakening, a shift. It's about more than just understanding or changing perspectives; it's about recognizing and embracing the choice to live differently, to live authentically.

And as we close this chapter, remember, I love you unconditionally. With each day that life unfolds, there are new opportunities to tailor your existence, to get things right for yourself.

So, I leave you with this hope: that you've awoken to your own narrative, that you've started crafting a life that's more consciously yours. Because in the end, waking up to your own world is the most profound journey you can embark on.

With unconditional love and an enduring hope for your awakening,

Django Degree, II

References

De Mello, Anthony. Awareness: Conversations with the Masters. Edited by J. Francis Stroud, Crown Publishing Group, 1990.

Drake. *For All The Dogs*. OVO Sound and Republic Records, 6 October 2023.

Hendrix, Harville. *Getting the Love You Want*. Pocket Books, 2005.

Kanye West & Jay Z. *Watch the Throne*. 8 August 2011.

Poet, Humble the. *How to Be Love(d): Simple Truths for Going Easier on Yourself, Embracing Imperfection & Loving Your Way to a Better Life*. Hay House, 2022.

Rumi, Jalal al-Din. *Mystical Poems of Rumi*. Edited by Ehsan Yarshater, translated by A. J. Arberry, University of Chicago Press, 2010.

Singer, Michael A. *The Untethered Soul: The Journey Beyond Yourself*. ReadHowYouWant.com, Limited, 2009.

Tolle, Eckhart. *The Power of Now: A Guide to Spiritual Enlightenment*. Hachette Australia, 2011.

Walker, Pete. *The Tao of Fully Feeling: Harvesting Forgiveness Out of Blame*. Azure Coyote Book, 2015.

Watts, Alan. *Behold the Spirit: A Study in the Necessity of Mystical Religion*. Knopf Doubleday Publishing Group, 1972.